Making the e-Business Transformation

Springer
London
Berlin
Heidelberg
New York
Barcelona
Hong Kong
Milan
Paris
Singapore
Tokyo

Peter Gloor

Making the e-Business Transformation

 Springer

Peter Gloor,
Zurich, Switzerland
gloor@acm.org

ISBN 1-85233-265-4 Springer-Verlag London Berlin Heidelberg

British Library Cataloguing in Publication Data
Gloor, Peter A. (Peter Andreas), 1961–
    Making the e-Business Transformation
    1. Business enterprises – Computer networks 2. Knowledge management
    I. Title
    658′.0546
    ISBN 1852332654

Library of Congress Cataloging-in-Publication Data
Gloor, Peter A. (Peter Andreas), 1961–
    Making the e-Business Transformation / Peter Gloor.
        p. cm.
    Includes bibliographical references and index.
    ISBN 1-85233-265-4 (alk. paper)
        1. electronic commerce. 2. Knowledge management. I. Title.
    HF5548.32 .G56 2000
    658′.054678–dc21   00-025095

Whilst we have made considerable efforts to contact all holders of copyright material contained in this book, we have failed to locate some of these. Should holders wish to contact the Publisher, we will be happy to come to some arrangement with them.

The use of registered names, trademarks etc. in this publication does not imply, even in the absence of a specific statement, that such names are exempt from the relevant laws and regulations and therefore free for general use.

The word "Allaire", the Allaire "A" logo, the "<allaire>" tag logo, the word ColdFusion and the ColdFusion "hand clutching lightning bolt" logo are registered trademarks of Allaire Corporation.

The publisher makes no representation, express or implied, with regard to the accuracy of the information contained in this book and cannot accept any legal responsibility or liability for any errors or omissions that may be made.

Typeset by Gray Publishing, Tunbridge Wells, Kent, England
Printed and bound at the Cromwell Press, Trowbridge, Wiltshire, England
34/3830-543210 Printed on acid-free paper SPIN 10755306

Acknowledgements

Fig. 2.16. © 1999, i2 Technologies, Inc.

Fig. 4.2. © 1998–2000 Allaire Corporation: used with permission of Allaire Corporation. All rights reserved.

Fig. 4.5. © World Wide Web Consortium (Massachusetts Institute of Technology, Institut National de Recherche en Informatique et en Automatique, Keio University). All rights reserved. http://www.w3.org/consortium.legal/

Fig. 4.8. and 4.9 © 1997–1999 Instinctive Technology, Inc. All rights reserved.

Figs. 4.10 and 4.11. © 2000 Lotus Development Corporation. Used with permission of Lotus Development Corporation. Instant!Teamroom and Sametime are trademarks of Lotus Development Corporation.

Fig. 4.21. © 1997–1999 Activeworlds.com, Inc.

Figs. 4.22 and 4.23. © 1998 RosettaNet. All rights reserved.

Fig. 5.12. © 1997–2000, Northern Light Technology Inc. All rights reserved.

Fig. 5.19. ThemeScape software is created and marketed by Cartia, Inc. (www.Cartia.com; www.newsmaps.com)

Fig. 5.20. © 1999 Semio corporation. All rights reserved. All artwork, logos and the names SemioMap, Semio Taxonomy and SemioBuilder are trademarks of Semio corporation.

Fig. 5.23. © 1999 Brøderbund Software. All rights reserved.

Contents

Introduction

Introduction	Definitions of: ▶ e-Commerce ▶ e-Business ▶ Knowledge management
1 Dispelling the myths of e-business	▶ Income gaps between industrialized countries and 3rd World ▶ Re-distribution of wealth in society ▶ Isolation of individual
2 Turning business into e-business	▶ e-Business transformation ▶ Business process outsourcing ▶ Portals ▶ Case study: pharmaceutical industry ▶ Case study: dating over the Web
3 Blueprint for e-business implementation	▶ The information process integration blueprint ▶ e-Business deployment roadmap ▶ Knowledge management deployment ▶ e-Business project management
4 Key e-business technologies	▶ XML overview ▶ Security and digital money ▶ Virtual collaboration ▶ Workflow management ▶ Process integration by packageware
5 Tools for managing knowledge	▶ MIT process handbook ▶ Knowledge navigation

> e-Business is approaching like a tidal wave: you must harness and use its power, or sooner or later you will be out of business!

e-Commerce, e-business and knowledge management are the enablers of rapid and fundamental change in the inner workings of enterprises and economies alike. If fully utilized they open up new areas for huge growth, the scale of which is unimaginable. This book shows to the managers of large and small businesses how they can react and adapt to the changes introduced by the explosive growth of the Internet.

The three main recommendations of this book are:

(1) To embrace technology early, be among the leaders and not the followers.
(2) To enable knowledge sharing in your company, by using appropriate knowledge-sharing tools, but more importantly, by supporting a culture that rewards the sharing and not the hoarding of knowledge.
(3) To reinvent new offerings based on your company's products by combining your own products with competing offerings.

The five chapters of this book address and answer key five questions.

Why is e-business the next great revolution in both business and society?

If we look at the time it has taken new technologies to dominate parts of our daily life, we see that the Internet has achieved this goal with an unprecedented speed. It has taken the radio about 38 years to be used by 50 million people. It has taken television about 13 years to reach the same number of people, but it has taken the Internet just 4 years to attract 50 million users (Fox, 1999).

The Internet is destined to change our life to an extent that we can not imagine today, with fundamental implications for all areas of business and society. Farsighted thinkers such as Michael Dertouzos (1997) from the Massachusetts Institute of Technology paint a picture where ubiquitously networked computers reach into all aspects of our daily life. In this book we will look at the consequences and implications of the Internet for the daily life of the individual and the company. We investigate how the Internet influences the way we communicate, collaborate, and work together in business and society.

How do you transform your business to e-business?

A company has two ways of adopting e-business, either doing a bottom-up e-business transformation or transforming itself into an e-business from the top down.

Using bottom-up e-business transformation, a company can automate its existing business processes by using e-business technologies such as document management, workflow systems, tools for collaboration, or packageware. This book lists a representative selection of sample processes, each particularly well suited for bottom-up e-business transformation.

A company is performing top-down e-business transformation if it fully embraces the new Internet-based economy, questioning its current strategy, and coming up with a new digital business model.

The current tendency for companies to stick to their core competencies favours outsourcing of all non-business critical activities. Internet technologies offer the ideal environment for business process outsourcing. The Web provides open standardized information access, seamlessly linking a company and its outsourcing provider.

A broad selection of case studies illustrates how leading firms have transformed their businesses. We single out the Web dating industry as a consistent early adopter of e-business technology, setting an example of a successful adaptation of all facets of Web technology.

How do you introduce e-business in your own company?

Once the decision has been made to embark on the journey towards e-business, there are many things that need to be considered. The first two chapters of the book focus the mindset of the e-business manager. Chapter 3 lists the obvious and less obvious steps on the e-business journey. It gives a high-level blueprint for the introduction of e-business-based business processes and the deployment of e-business technology, based on the practical project experience of the author in various leadership functions in the e-business consulting practices of global management consulting firms.

What are the key enabling technologies?

e-Business and e-commerce represent a revolution brought about by information technology. While computers and computer networks have been around for the past 50 years, it is only in the past 5 years that these have found their way into our everyday life. In Chapter 4 we will look at the key technology enablers for the e-business company to succeed in the e-commerce economy.

While there are hot new technologies such as neural networks, fuzzy logic, and intelligent autonomous agents, the corporate IT environment exhibits a growing tendency towards software packages. Essential business processes such as building customer loyalty, reaching new markets, creating new products and services, enhancing human capital, and managing risk and compliance have been automated in the past using custom-built client/server applications written in programming languages such as COBOL, C, Pascal, FoxPro, etc. Today these business processes are increasingly automated with out-of-the-box software packages. This means, for example, that not only are well-structured internal enterprise resource planning processes supported by tools from SAP or Peoplesoft, but also much more flexible and unstructured processes such as client-relationship management are increasingly supported by tailorable off-the-shelf packageware systems from Siebel, Vantive or Broadvision among others.

Business process redesign (BPR) topped the agenda of most Fortune 500 companies during the better part of the 1990s. Workflow management, the automatic control of well-structured business processes, has held great promise as the engine of BPR. Unfortunately, until now, workflow management tools have not been able to deliver on that promise. While there are dozens of dedicated workflow engines, the breakthrough for this technology has yet to come. There are few "pure" workflow implementations on a global scale. The workflow concept is mainly used by packageware: reengineered business processes are being implemented by customizable enterprise resource planning (ERP), sales force automation, or e-procurement packages.

What are the tools for managing domain and process knowledge?

Of particular importance are the IT tools available for making knowledge accessible. While there are collaboration and information retrieval tools such as Lotus Notes, currently no off-the-shelf packages exist that cover all aspects of knowledge management. This book identifies the knowledge navigation and visualization concepts and describes the tools and concepts for building state-of-the art knowledge management systems.

To be able to reengineer business processes, a company needs to know first what its current business processes are. Obtaining a high-level overview of these processes is a far from trivial task. Once the current processes are known, a company can then get to work to completely reengineer those processes, preferably benchmarking the redesigned processes with the best-in-class processes of the leader in the company's business domain. The Process Handbook project was started by Professor Tom Malone about 8 years ago at MIT's Sloan School of Management. Its goal is to build a repository of business processes covering a broad range of industries and activities. Towards that goal, the Process Handbook project has also come up with a patented way for describing, comparing, and measuring processes. At this point, more than 5000 business processes have been captured in leading banking, pharmaceutical, oil and electronics companies, plus many other companies, covering activities such as product development, production, and marketing and sales.

e-Business and knowledge management

In the days of the mainframe, only a small, mostly white-collar fraction of the workforce used computers, i.e. terminals, at their workplace. In the days of the client/server applications, the percentage changed somewhat, in that a slightly larger group were given PCs on their desks to support their office work. But only very recently, with the stellar rise of the Internet and its associated technologies, has the computer and information technology penetrated all aspects of business life (Fig. I.1). The waiter in the restaurant, the supermarket clerk, even farmers and chimney-sweeps are using portable, hand-held computers. At work, the majority of workers are in daily contact with the computer. It is already considered a common expectation of every school child in the Western world to have access to the Internet and the World Wide Web!

e-Business covers the application of Internet technology in all aspects of the business world. It is frequently used in the limited sense of consumers buying goods over the Internet from vendors displaying their offerings on their Web site. In this book we use the term "e-business" in the broader meaning of using Internet-based information technology along the whole value chain, from the producer of raw goods, through the various manufacturers, up to the consumer. A company can communicate with its business partners over an *Extranet* network using Internet-technology with the Extranet behaving like a dedicated wide area network. The *Intranet* is an Internet confined to the boundaries of the corporation.

We use the term *e-commerce* for the activities of marketing, selling, and buying of products and services on the Internet. e-Business, on the other hand, is improving business performance through connectivity by deploying Internet technologies in the value chain over Internet, Intranet, and Extranet to achieve dramatic improvements in quality and quantity (Fig. I.2). e-Business connects the value chain between and across businesses; and between business and

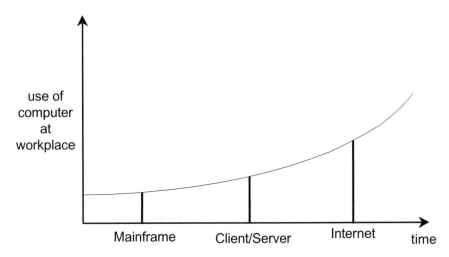

Fig. I.1.   Penetration of computers at the workplace.

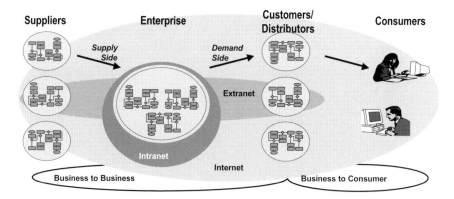

Fig. I.2.   Carrying out e-business and e-commerce over Internet, Intranet, and Extranet (source: Deloitte Consulting).

consumers to get better service and to reduce cost. It also opens up new channels, thereby transforming competitive landscapes.

e-Business is the integration of processes, organizations and systems through Internet-based and related technologies, to create differentiated business value and competitive positions. From a technological viewpoint, e-business and e-commerce make use of a vast collection of IT concepts and tools, such as ERP, Datawarehousing, workflow/workgroup, customer relationship management, ECR (efficient consumer response), sales force automation, call centres, document management, and so on (Fig. I.3). Open Internet standards such as TCP/IP, HTML, WWW, XML, Java, CORBA, etc. are used to integrate and automate the value chain by providing a common language for systems to transparently interface between processes and to exchange data.

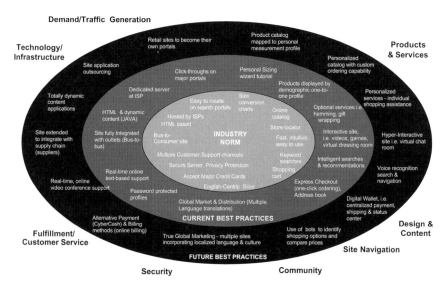

Fig. I.3.   Technologies associated with e-business (source: Deloitte Consulting).

In its first 2 years of existence, e-business has already come a long way from being a smiled-at buzzword of technophobes to having far-reaching implications in the everyday live of everybody in the industrialized world.

In today's extremely competitive business landscape, only the company that successfully applies e-business technologies to managing knowledge in all aspects of its dealings with clients, business partners, and its own employees will be prosperous. Dell Computer is an example of managing knowledge for customer experiences using leading edge e-business systems. Michael Dell, Dell Computer's founder and CEO has clearly formulated his vision: "At Dell, we believe the customer is in control, and our job is to take all the technology that's out there and apply it in a useful way to meet the customer's needs". Dell Computer has $18.2 billion in sales with a 48% compound annual growth, and $1.5 billion in profits with an even more spectacular 55% annual growth. It was the top performing stock of the 1990s with a market capitalization of $109 billion. Dell is characterized by its success in specializing in custom-made computers. It co-creates and extends its products and services through customer partnerships. Its production is virtually integrated along the value chain for speed, flexibility and profitability. Dell sets a prime example for managing its process knowledge by using the latest e-business technology.

In this book we distinguish between data, information, and knowledge, using the definitions given by knowledge management expert Davenport (Davenport and Prusak, 1997).

- *Data* consist of sets of discrete *objective facts about events*. Typically they are in the form of structured records of transactions. There is no inherent meaning in data records.
- *Information* is called by Davenport *"data that makes a difference"*. Information can be thought of being sent in a message. The receiver who gets the message decides whether its information has a meaning or not.
- *Knowledge*, according to Davenport, *"derives from minds at work"*. It is a framework for evaluating and incorporating new experiences and information. It is embedded not only in documents, but also in

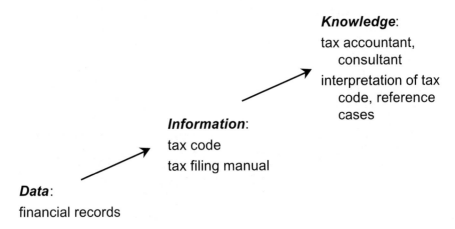

Fig. I.4. From data to information to knowledge.

organizational routines and processes. Knowledge is only valuable in context: a medical textbook is only of value for a trained physician; the best medical textbook does not make a medical layperson a doctor.

For an example, look at how we fill out our tax forms: we collect *data*, in the form of our financial records, income declarations, or banking statements. We search for *information*, in the form of tax codes, or tax filing manuals. If our financial situation is complicated, we consult a tax expert, whose accumulated *knowledge* about tax codes, reference cases, and local tax specialties helps to optimally fill out our tax forms.

There are two types of knowledge: explicit knowledge and tacit knowledge. *Explicit* knowledge is documented information that can facilitate action. It is packaged, communicable, transferable, and can be expressed in a formal, shared language. It can be formulas or equations written in a book, a description of a business process, a blueprint for semiconductor production, or a procedures and policies manual for a company. *Tacit* knowledge is much harder to capture: It is know-how and learning embedded within the "heads and bodies" of the people in the organization. It is personal, context-specific, hard to formalize, hard to communicate, and much more difficult to transfer. It consists of skills and beliefs, of values, of perceptions, insights, and experiences, of mental models and patterns. Knowledge originates from individuals and is embodied in teams and organizations. An organization combines explicit knowledge about strategies, methodologies, core competencies, processes, patents, and products and services with tacit knowledge about customers, account management approaches, values and culture. A team incorporates explicit knowledge about practices and procedures, functional and cross-functional know-how, and tacit knowledge about team norms and collaborative approaches. Individuals in the organization contribute tacit knowledge such as their skills and competency, their experiences, their relationships within and outside the organization, their beliefs and values, and their ideas.

Knowledge is embedded within work processes and exists in all core processes of an organization. For example, strategic planning processes incorporate knowledge about the intent behind the chosen strategic direction and learnings from past strategies. Sales and marketing processes contain knowledge about the best way to position products and services, or feedback from the CEO of a key customer account. Customer care processes embody knowledge about why customers don't buy more of the company's product or some key product flaws. A human resources process can include knowledge about how to best mentor new engineers, while a financial process could incorporate knowledge about earnings on new products.

It is critical to view processes from a knowledge perspective, looking beyond task-based information management. Key decisions are made in each step of a business process, both explicit knowledge and tacit knowledge are required to make effective decisions. This view has implications for performance support and process innovation.

Knowledge management caters for the critical issues of organizational adaptation and competence in these times of increasing change on all levels. It embodies organizational processes that seek synergistic combinations of data and information processing capabilities, of information technologies, and of the creative and innovative capacity of human beings.*

The full benefits of e-business can only be reaped if the knowledge involved in each e-business process is appropriately managed. This means that knowing about processes and background information is absolutely key for everybody participating in e-commerce and e-business, be it a potter in Zimbabwe or a large multinational "best-of-class" corporation such as Dell, Wall-Mart, or Microsoft.

Davenport (Davenport and Prusak, 1997) calls knowledge the main asset of a corporation. This book makes the argument that successful companies in today's competitive and fast-paced fast-changing e-business landscape will not only manage knowledge, but willingly and openly **share knowledge**, albeit by being fairly compensated for it. For an obvious example, look at Apple, the microcomputer manufacturer: Apple would have had a major advantage had it licensed its operating system on to the Intel chip set in 1988 instead of locking it onto its proprietary hardware. Other, easily found examples abound: The patent system was invented to make sharing of knowledge profitable to the inventor of a novel idea.

Leading companies in today's e-business world have succeeded because they made better use of knowledge. Wal-Mart has produced stellar results in the most mundane of industries: mass merchandising, where margins are low and competition is ferocious. Wal-Mart won by exploiting general aviation, multimedia networking, and computerized inventory control and fleet management to become one of the fastest growing and most profitable companies in the world.

The Internet makes information accessible to everyone. Unfortunately, the fact that the information is out there, somewhere, does not yet mean that it can be used productively. To create knowledge out of information is a far from trivial matter. In the e-business economy, knowledge becomes the main asset. The company that puts knowledge to the best use will gain the most.

Knowledge facilitation, also called "intermediation", is the new business model, which is typical of the e-business economy. The knowledge facilitator, the intermediary, is the one who knows that:

- X knows a certain fact;
- Y has a certain skill;
- Z is looking for a certain item.

Intermediaries that collect information and make it accessible will be the ones profiting the most by e-business. e-Business high-flyers Amazon.com (mass customized commodity selling and auctioning) and eBay.com (virtual auctioning), as well as on-line dating communities such as Match.com, Friendfinder.com, etc. are typical of this new kind of knowledge broker company.

Even in this globally networked e-business world where the computer reaches into every aspect of daily business and private life, the human element

---

*Knowledge management should not be confused with artificial intelligence, where the goal is to make computers intelligent enough to be able to solve the same problems as human beings.

is still the most crucial. Companies that have successfully combined the latest Internet technology with the human element are gaining the most. Amazon, eBay, and Dell Computer, as well as Web dating companies, have all combined different seemingly unrelated business areas to offer new services that were not thought of and impossible to provide in the pre-e-business era.

"The sheer reach and structural complexity of the Web makes it an ecology of knowledge, with relationships, information 'food chains,' and dynamic interactions that could soon become as rich as, if not richer than, many natural ecosystems," Dr. Huberman from the world-famous Xerox PARC Research Center wrote in a paper last year with his colleagues Peter Pirolli, James Pitkow and Rajan Lukose.

But it is hard to find the right metaphor for something so strange. Viewed in real time, with data seekers buzzing from site to site, the Web can seem like a swarm of virtual insects, one whose flutterings (in the form of mouse clicks) can be recorded and sifted for clues to behavioral laws.

"We are not doing computer science," Dr. Huberman said, "but something more akin to social science." What strategies do people use to hunt down information? Why, for no apparent reason, do storms of activity suddenly surge through the Internet, causing the whole thing to come to a halt? And why, just as mysteriously, do these information fronts suddenly subside?

Ever since the Web began to burgeon, barely under human control, people have been straining to relate it to something familiar – an ecosystem, the weather, an unruly crowd at a rock concert. The Web is a great ocean on which you surf from site to site. It's a cyberspace with a topology of its own: Two points distant in physical space can be adjacent in cyberspace, a single mouse click away. But an e-mail message sent in an instant to a neighbor next door might be routed through a maze of links extending thousands of miles.

Lada Adamic, a Stanford University graduate student working on Xerox PARC's Internet ecology project, recently found that cyberspace, like the world described in the John Guare play "Six Degrees of Separation," is a small place indeed. Just as any two people on Earth are said to be connected by a human chain of acquaintance with no more than a few links, so can you pick two Web sites at random and get from one to the other with about four clicks.

The research quantifies what Web users intuitively know: Because of the high density of connections, it can be surprisingly easy to find information in what amounts to a library without a card catalog, filled with unindexed books.

The thunderstorms of congestion on the Net, another study found, can be analyzed in terms of crowd behavior. Sudden clots of congestion can sometimes be traced to obvious causes, like the recent virtual lingerie show of Victoria's Secret. More often they arise and quickly dissipate for obscure reasons best understood using what social scientists call game theory.

Searching for the Essence of the World Wide Web by George Johnson, April 11 1999. Copyright © 1999 The New York Times Co. Reprinted with permission.

This citation from a *New York Times* article paints a colourful picture of a world, society, and economy extensively influenced by the Internet. It depicts a world that has embarked on a course of rapid change, enabled by the Internet. Where this change will end, how our world will look in 20 years from now is impossible to say. The only thing which is certain is that it will be thoroughly different, and that computers, networks and the Internet will play an increasingly dominating role.

In my own work as a management consultant advising leading global companies, the Internet and e-business has become the driver for change, sending those companies on a fascinating journey whose end is absolutely open. This book shows today's business managers not only how to survive in this fast-paced environment, but also how to harness the full potential of Internet technology by turning their businesses into e-businesses.

Roadmap

Chapter 1 discusses the common myths of e-business. The conclusion is that although the individual, the society, the economy, and the company are all put at risk by e-business, the potential rewards are worth that risk.

Chapter 2 looks at how a company can fully leverage the potential benefits of the Internet age to transform itself into an e-business. The conclusion is that it is essential to be a technology leader, to be prepared to share knowledge within the company as well as with competitors, and to come up with products that draw on emotions.

Chapter 3 describes how the e-business transformation project within a company should be managed. The conclusion is that e-business projects are software projects that need to be managed using state-of-the-art software engineering methods. The problem is that e-business projects need to be completed with far greater speed than previous projects, which requires the use of standard software packages where possible.

Chapter 4 gives an in-depth technical discussion of all the main e-business technologies that enable a company to become an e-business. While the technologies are manifold, emphasis needs to be put on reliability, scalability, and security.

Chapter 5 describes tools for managing process and domain knowledge in a company. While there are no clear leaders in this field, there are promising systems that give early adapters a head start against the competition.

Acknowledgements

I am deeply grateful to Cathy Benko, Global Practice Leader e-business of Deloitte Consulting, for finding time in her busy schedule to thoroughly review this manuscript and to make invaluable suggestions. I also thank my colleagues from Deloitte Consulting, Gilbert Toppin, Chair e-business Council Europe, and Pawel Paukert, Niki Flandorfer, Markus Hegi, and Laura Ghezzi for giving me input on the latest developments in the e-business space.

Paul Biggs and Philipp Indlekofer also provided valuable comments.

I would like to thank PricewaterhouseCoopers for financing my 6-month sabbatical to write this book. Special thanks go to Peter Weibel, Senior Partner of PricewaterhouseCoopers Switzerland, to Eric Nef, Partner, Head of IT/ Systems Integration of PricewaterhouseCoopers Switzerland, and to Bruno Nell, former Head of IT/Systems Integration of what was at that time STG Coopers & Lybrand Switzerland.

I would also like to thank my friends Marc Brown from Ariba, James (Chuck) Davin, CTO of PSI, and David Tennenhouse, director of the Information Technology Office at DARPA, for introducing me to the inside of their organizations. I am deeply indebted to Fillia Makedon from the Department of Computer Science at Dartmouth College for the long and fruitful cooperation that started well before the e-business era. I am very grateful to Tom Malone for sharing his insights about the Process Handbook and for letting me into the Process Handbook team. I would also like to thank Dr Steinhardt, Roche, Dr Frei, Zurich Insurance, and Herman Blaser, Generali Insurance, for their collaboration.

Special thanks go to my good friends Susan Wood and Andre Ruedi for commenting on early drafts of the book manuscript and suggesting this book title.

Do e-business or die!

1 *Dispelling the myths of e-business*

Introduction	Definitions of: ▶ e-Commerce ▶ e-Business ▶ Knowledge management
1 Dispelling the myths of e-business	**▶ Income gaps between industrialized countries and 3rd World** **▶ Re-distribution of wealth in society** **▶ Isolation of individual**
2 Turning business into e-business	▶ e-Business transformation ▶ Business process outsourcing ▶ Portals ▶ Case study: pharmaceutical industry ▶ Case study: dating over the Web
3 Blueprint for e-business implementation	▶ The information process integration blueprint ▶ e-Business deployment roadmap ▶ Knowledge management deployment ▶ e-Business project management
4 Key e-business technologies	▶ XML overview ▶ Security and digital money ▶ Virtual collaboration ▶ Workflow management ▶ Process integration by packageware
5 Tools for managing knowledge	▶ MIT process handbook ▶ Knowledge navigation

> This chapter looks at familiar myths and beliefs associated with the global dissemination of the Internet. It analyzes and challenges the opportunities of e-business for society, business, and the individual.

The e-business economy has gained an unstoppable momentum. Computers and the Internet now reach into all aspects of our daily life. Farmers on remote islands control their cattle-feed by computers, mass-tailored underwear is sold over the Web, and grandparents stay in touch with their grandchildren by e-mail.

Multinational corporations are using the Internet and e-business as an integral tool for daily work. Increasingly, small- and medium-sized enterprises have to understand the implications of e-business for their company and to be able to use it to offer better services, reduce their production costs, and link to business partners and customers. Businesses of any size need to adapt to e-business and e-commerce, or they will be overtaken by their more flexible competitors. Like the steam engine, the railway, the car, the telephone, the TV, and the computer, e-commerce and e-business will have a fundamental impact on the business landscape, forever changing the way in which business is done. The Internet and e-business is bringing unprecedented wealth and a period of rapid economic growth to the industrialized world. The countries that most ardently embrace e-business will see the biggest gains, with the most fervent adopter being the biggest winner, currently the USA.

While individuals, corporations and governments alike are excited about the thrilling prospects of e-business and e-commerce, there are undoubtedly risks associated with this new electronic world. It is therefore well worth taking one step back in order to look at the hazards that can potentially turn the promised benefits of e-business into disadvantages.

In this first chapter we will identify the biggest challenges that e-business poses to society, business, and the individual. We will then show how the associated risks can be turned into opportunities for further profit. From this analysis we can draw valuable lessons, equally valid for the e-business transformation in any company, independent of its industry.

1.1 e-Commerce widens the income gap between the developed and the developing world?

Electronic business opens a gigantic, world-wide decentralized market with low transaction costs and little entry barriers. This will transform structures of traditional markets and will have a dramatic impact on producers, distribution channels and the labour market. For the first time in history, a genuine global market is becoming reality, independent of the tiresome discussions on opening national markets or of the painstaking efforts towards liberalization – electronic business is "born global".

This rapid integration of electronic trade is coupled with the large risk that the North–South gap between rich and poor will be widened. Instead of helping in closing the income disparity between industrialized and developing countries, e-commerce threatens to widen the gap. Although there are laudable efforts by the United Nations and other governmental and non-governmental development agencies to utilize the potential of e-commerce to support enterprises in developing countries, the hurdles and obstacles for individuals and for small businesses in the third world to profit from e-business are almost insurmountable. Many governments in poorer countries have difficulties funding programs to facilitate the trade between other countries around the globe – especially in countries where poor telecommunications leave less scope for new technologies. Wireless technologies have the promise to catapult countries with poorly developed physical networks directly into the Internet age, but satellite-based Internet connections in poor rural areas in developing countries are still only available for a small group of select pilot communities financed by Western donor countries. To further reduce the gap, UNCTAD (United Nations Conference on Trade and Development), for instance, proposed a world-wide network of Trade Points to support e-commerce.

The UN Trade Point Program

The Trade Point Program was initiated by UNCTAD in 1992. The objective is to assist small- and medium-sized enterprises (SMEs) in overcoming the informational, financial and logistic obstacles to increased participation in international trade, with a particular emphasis on firms in developing and transitional economies. Trade Points attempt to bring together under one roof all the services needed by exporters: government offices, customs authorities, chambers of commerce, banks, insurers, and freight forwarders, etc. Trade Points enable SMEs to use the Internet and services such as EDI or Web homepages to gain access to computerized information on markets, potential clients and potential investors, tariffs and trade rules world-wide. This 'one-stop-shopping' should lower transaction costs of importing and exporting. It also reduces the obstacles to trade, thus encouraging new entrants into the trade arena.

By 1997, the number of Trade Points in operation or under development had reached 136 – located in developing and transitional economies as well as in numerous industrialized countries. Their service and technology capabilities generally reflect the present limits of the local business environment and related institutional constraints. For example, many Trade Points in the least developed countries have minimal Internet access while some of their counterparts in advanced countries operate "virtual Trade Points" where most of their information and service resources are available on the Web. The most remarkable service of the Trade Point Network is the Internet-based ETOs (electronic trade opportunities). Allegedly this is the largest database of requests for offers, bids, and other kinds of business transactions disseminated electronically.

The organizational forms employed vary widely across the network. Some Trade Points are government-run institutions or are largely state-supported while others are non-profit institutions, private companies or affiliates of economic development organizations. Other programs by the WTO and other organizations have tackled similar issues. Unfortunately, overall transparency is lacking. Reports on the low effectiveness and efficiency of these programs have sparked discussion on which model is the most appropriate, and if this huge "inter-governmental machinery" should play a role at all in the e-business arena. The alternative would be to leave all initiatives to the free market.

"Virtualization" of the Trade Point system

When the Trade Point Program was initially conceived in 1992, it was intended that Trade Points would operate as "one-stop-shops", providing all the necessary trade information and ancillary services needed to conduct international trade transactions, such as arrangement of custom, financing, transport and insurance, at one location. I had the chance to visit selected Trade Points on behalf of the United Nations in fall 1998. On the site visits we got a rather diverse picture: A number of Trade Points only provide trade information, while others offer a comprehensive set of services – such as customs clearance, banking and freight forwarding – under one roof, as initially conceived. In some Trade Points the various service providers maintain a physical presence at one location, while in others (e.g. Trade Point Beijing) an EDI network links together the various partners electronically. Overall, there appear to be four major variants of Trade Points (Fig. 1.1).

(1) Physical Trade Information Trade Point – These Trade Points either provide only trade information and communication facilities (e.g. photocopier, Internet access) or bring together under one roof service providers such as banks, insurance companies and freight forwarders who can advise clients on how to carry out their trade transactions. The actual transactional services are furnished outside of the Trade Point in the service provider's offices.

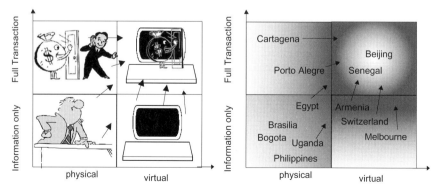

Fig. 1.1 Trade Points are becoming virtual.

(2) Physical Trade Facilitation Trade Point – This form of Trade Point offers trade information, advice and counselling, banking services, access to customs, and shipping services on its premises so that clients can arrange all the details of their transaction in one location.
(3) Virtual Trade Information Trade Point – A Virtual Trade Point generally offers trade information and Internet-based trading services through a Web site. This type of Trade Point, in most cases, also has physical offices but does not generally host representatives of affiliated trade service providers. However, their Web site may contain a trade services directory or hyperlinks to the Web sites of its partner organizations.
(4) Virtual Trade Facilitation Trade Point – A virtual Trade Point brings together its affiliated service providers using EDI over the Internet or a private network. A Trade Point client can exchange transaction information with the trade services providers on-line, either from the Trade Point's offices or from their own premises if they have the requisite communications capabilities. In most developing countries these Trade Points also have physical offices.

Depending on the degree of development of the local economy, most Trade Points are moving towards this last mode of operation, i.e. the virtual trade facilitation Trade Point. They are progressing more or less rapidly, depending on the degree of trade development within the local economy. Countries with less advanced technological infrastructure or insufficient demand for international trade services normally have limited telecommunications infrastructure; therefore it is not possible for local enterprises to have computer networks and Internet access. Furthermore, enterprises in these countries cannot afford the cost of computers and Internet access. In such countries the emphasis is put on physically providing trade information and facilitation services. For example, Internet-based trading information is reviewed by the Trade Point staff and forwarded to relevant clients in the form of periodic paper-hardcopy bulletins. Governments typically play a key role in terms of providing funding and other resources. Countries in black Africa usually fall into this category.

In highly industrialized countries physical "one-stop-shops" are becoming obsolete, as information and access to services are readily available through various information channels. Many Trade Points in advanced economies have attempted to package a suite of free and fee-based information as well as facilitation services, which are delivered through a Web site.

On my Trade Point site visits I had the opportunity to collect first-hand experience on the progress of e-business in different countries in various stages of economic development.

China

In 1994, the Chinese government launched the four "Golden Programs", namely the "Golden Bridge" – an information highway, the "Golden Gate" – a paperless trading system, the "Golden Card" – a national credit card processing system, and the "Golden Tax" – a computerized tax system. The Golden Gate program aims to build up an integrated e-commerce system by connecting traders, enterprises, and government agencies involved in foreign trade to a network and to develop special software for processing foreign trade transactions.

Chinese Trade Points want to provide the full set of e-commerce services:

- Virtual fairs and on-line malls to present goods and services.
- Fully support the sales and buy process by extending the ETO system to include a negotiation and price-finding cycle as well as full user authentication.
- Support the payment process over the Internet.

China has two types of Trade Points. Large "official UN" Trade Points following the one-stop-shop concept are located in Beijing and Shanghai. They offer the full set of trade information, trade facilitation, and trade transaction services under one roof. The second type of Trade Points began in 1997 when the Chinese initiated a new "unofficial" Trade Point concept. Currently, virtual trading points have been set up in 30 Chinese cities covering main trading centres. They consist of a physical access point, i.e. an office, that provides the Chinese export companies with Internet access to trade information, trade facilitation, and trade transaction services. The service providers such as banks, insurers, freight forwarders, etc. are no longer located under the same roof as the Trade Point, but provide their services over the Internet.

The Chinese Ministry of Foreign Trade and Economic Cooperation (MOFTEC) is responsible for launching this Chinese e-commerce initiative. MOFTEC operates the web site moftec.gov.cn, which is open to all registered importing and exporting Chinese companies, but is used only by a fraction.

MOFTEC operators scan all the electronic trading opportunities (ETOs) coming in over the Internet and translate the ones considered relevant for China using an automatic translation system. China also participates in a UN-sponsored digital certificate infrastructure initiative. The digital certificate system grants authentication certificates to the importing and exporting companies registered at the Trade Point. At the end of 1996 the development of a secure ETO system was assigned to MOFTEC by the UN.

Brazil

The recent deregulation of Brazil's telecommunication market has backed the rapid national success of the Internet. Almost 500 Internet Service Providers (ISPs) and over 500,000 Internet-host computers are providing a wide range of services to a growing community of Brazilian Internet users (8 million periodical users in 1998). Brazil has the largest and most developed Trade Point network world-wide, with 11 operational Trade Points and another two in the process of becoming operational. The Brazilian Trade Points are run by government, semi-private, and private organizations. The semi-private Brazilian export promotion agency SEBRAE plays a significant role as one of the main national sponsors of the Trade Point program participating in almost every Trade Point.

It is one of the Brazilian national priorities to double exports in the next 5 years. Therefore local chambers of commerce and the Brazilian government are willing to cover operating costs and to finance an adequate infrastructure of the Trade Point system. Nevertheless, it is the ambition of most Trade Point directors to become self-sustained in the medium term by charging customers directly for the services provided. Some services are already provided for a nominal fee, but that is mostly because "free services are not worth anything". The Brazilian government closely monitors its Trade Points and sponsors a national Trade Point Forum, where all Brazilian Trade Point directors meet on a quarterly basis. Brazil is also the main sponsor of the regional Latin American Trade Point federation. The Brazilian national agency for improving trade efficiency has just started a Web site, BrazilTradeNet, which links the various Trade Points. BrazilTradeNet provides export-related information such as searchable directories of Brazilian firms and foreign firms willing to invest in Brazil, as well as a browser-based ETO-compatible system to send and receive actual trade and investment opportunities.

Senegal

In Africa the liberalization of the telecommunication market is still in its infancy. The reason is a conflict of interest: In most African countries telecommunication companies are still state-owned. While governments are responsible for setting up the regulatory framework for privatization, liberalization and deregulation, they remain interested in the revenue 'their' carrier provides. For the vast majority of Africans, access to phone lines, fax or Internet is extremely constrained.

According to the UN Economic Council of Africa (ECA) 35 out of 49 countries where one phone line is shared by more than 100 inhabitants are African. Furthermore, bad connection quality compounds the problem of using a phone or fax for business purposes. Although Internet technology has considerable advantages for transmission over poor quality lines, Internet access remains a luxury. In Kenya, for example, eight Internet Service Providers (ISP) provide approximately 15,000 customers with access to the Internet. The monthly charge is between $100 and $200. With respect to the average yearly income of $300 this is prohibitively expensive (WER, 1998). The membership in the exclusive Windsor golf club in Nairobi is three times less expensive!

Some countries are successfully implementing trade promotion facilities, which will have a considerable impact on the local economy. Senegal, for instance, managed to unify almost all "components" of the import or export processes into a networked solution developed by the Trade Point Dakar. Any producer or trader is able to enter the necessary formalities once, instead of filling in 20 different paper forms. Using the new system, they can electronically track the progress of their request through all stages, covering customs, export insurance, bank credit, veterinary or health services, freight forwarders, and many others. This service is not restricted to the economic centre of Senegal, but is made available to rural regions using the existing infrastructure of postal offices, playing the role of "Internet Café's". The result are reduced transaction times and costs by streamlining processes for interconnecting trading parties and rapid access to important trade-related information.

Egypt

Egypt has quite a large well-educated workforce and a rather advanced infrastructure. As a result, networked computers are widely used to conduct business in Egypt. Also, the Internet has started to be used not only as a trade promotion device, but to actually conduct trade. For example, the state-financed Egypt Trade Point department has about 130 employees. The main Trade Point in Cairo operates an extensive one-stop-shop with customs, banking and insurance, air transportation, marine transportation, foreign trade regulations, and trade research services. The Trade Point makes intensive use of IT, all data is stored in computerized databases, which are maintained by 30 programmers in the IT group of the Trade Point. A project to create a unified database is on the way. Customer data as well as the information needed to answer queries are kept and continually updated in customized databases. The Trade Point also successfully developed a multimedia CD to market the products of its clients.

Philippines

Contrarily to other emerging economies, Internet access is not very advanced in the Philippines. Out of the 2000 exporters in the government exporter database, only 20 had e-mail addresses in fall 1998. On my visit, Philippine government officials estimated (probably somewhat generously) that about 40% of the Philippine households could afford to buy a computer. The general problem with skilled Philippine computer programmers is that they are hired away to the USA.

In contrast to the other countries I visited, the Trade Point program has not been a big success in the Philippines. Reasons for the failure of the Trade Point program in the Philippines could be:

- The Philippine Chamber of Commerce, where the Trade Point is currently located, is too profit oriented. Countries where the Trade Points have been a full success execute more state control over their economies. In free market economies, such as the Philippines, where the initiative is up to the private sector there is not enough profit to be made with Trade Points.
- The Philippine government (the Department of Trade and Industry) provides very little coordination and guidance between competing trade promotion organizations.
- There are already enough other trade promotion organizations and systems in place that do the Trade Point's job.

If we compare the Philippines with more "dirigistic" countries like Brazil or China, it seems that the Trade Point concept and the adaptation of e-commerce have been more successful in advanced developing countries. Additionally, governments that have decisively invested in building up an e-commerce hardware and software infrastructure have helped to make their enterprises more productive. Governments in developing countries with a "laissez-faire" attitude have achieved mixed results in e-commerce progress.

Improving e-business dissemination

In an interview a senior representative of the Ministry of Trade and Industry in a lesser developed country expressed concerns which in my view most governments share. Public-policy-makers fear that the high degree of change and the speed of e-commerce may weaken their influence, which they exercise by regulating the establishment of businesses, customs or through taxation. Besides concern about the applicability of existing policies or the need for new rules, policy-makers also do not yet fully understand the impact that this new form of commerce will have on employment, productivity, trade and growth. Will e-commerce and e-business lead to the substitution of new, less labour-intensive intermediaries for traditional distribution? Will the resulting savings lead to lower prices? Will e-commerce continue to erode the ability to track international trade, and thus weaken the ability to measure GDP and its growth? Will it even remove the base for collecting taxes?

The momentum triggered by e-business has led governments to become more market-minded in spite of uncertainties. But there is still much debate about where and how political and commercial responsibilities need to be separated. These developments present governments with new opportunities but also mean new challenges, as they may alter the traditional relationship with their citizens and with other states.

To improve the dissemination of e-business in developing countries and to afford all countries similar chances to profit from the e-business revolution, a differentiated approach should be pursued. It must be distinguishing between "advanced" developing countries that can build on local strengths and "least" developed countries. In "advanced" developing countries the local e-business infrastructure should be built-up rapidly. Industrialized Western countries should support the construction of this Internet infrastructure in their own interest, to get access to these emerging markets as well as access to a large pool of well-educated computer specialists. For "least" developed countries (LDCs), a different approach should be employed, providing startup support. For instance, the UN is offering Internet incubator services, operating the infrastructure including networks and Web servers on behalf of the developing countries, also training local personnel to operate this infrastructure in the near future.

Training in e-business-related disciplines is absolutely crucial for both advanced developing countries and LDCs. The goal should be to "train the trainers", to train local teachers in Internet technology and e-business topics and to develop distance-learning materials for traders and end users in developing countries.

Besides well-educated users capable of using a computer and connecting it to the Internet, the appropriate infrastructure also needs to be set up. Western countries should assist in building up the Internet infrastructure and e-commerce trading systems, for example developing a secure electronic trading opportunity system such as the SETO system described later in this book. This should include the development of mechanisms to securely transfer micro-payments over the Internet.

Another crucial issue is legislation and deregulation. Laws are frequently inadequate for electronic trading, and customs officials are ill equipped to deal with goods that are being sold internationally over the Internet. The telecom carriers in developing countries are frequently still monopolized, resulting in an inefficient infrastructure and high access prices. Competition has to be introduced to lower infrastructure access costs.

To set up an Internet infrastructure and to start wide-ranging training programs requires substantial investment. Developing countries are unable to come up with startup financing, which means that without donor seed funding developing countries are unable to get started and will definitively be left out of the e-business economy. The rich Western industrialized countries should, for their own interests, assist by providing funding for training and setting up an adequate telecommunications infrastructure. Otherwise, the split between rich and poor will rapidly expand, locking out 80% of the world's population from the benefits of e-business, and also depriving the Western economy of a large and widely untapped market and labour resource potential.

After this discussion of the impact of e-business for the third world, let's look at what e-business means for the society in the industrialized world.

1.2   e-Business squares the bell curve?

Richard Herrnstein and Charles Murray suggest in their heavily disputed book *The Bell Curve: Intelligence and Class Structure in American Life* (1996) a new aristocracy of the intellect, where intelligent people will marry among themselves, producing even more intelligent offspring. These increasingly intelligent people will further dominate the Western world. Herrnstein and Murray argue that intelligence, and not environmental circumstances, poverty, or lack of education are at the root of individual success. If Herrnstein and Murray are correct, then e-business will accelerate this trend, because making full use of the potential of e-business undoubtedly requires a high IQ. Only intelligent (and thus already successful) individuals can master the complexity of e-business. This would mean that e-business would help in making the rich (the more intelligent) richer, and the poor poorer, widening the gap between haves and have-nots. In short, e-business could divide society.

I have a much more optimistic view. e-Business has the potential to be a big equalizer, providing uniform information access for everyone, to everyone. Underprivileged groups of society can get global information access. Each individual has the same opportunity to get the information he or she is looking for regardless of whether they are living in an affluent metropolitan or suburban area or in a rural backwater area. Small- and medium-sized enterprises (SMEs) in disadvantaged (remote) regions get a chance to compete globally against multinationals, thus spreading wealth into remote regions. Managing a global company has become much cheaper, because global information networks can now be operated as Extranets for a fraction of the price of dedicated leased lines. International trade barriers become obsolete, not only for immaterial goods, but also for material goods. Global freighting companies such as FedEx or UPS can operate much more efficiently thanks to the Internet, shipping to remote locations for a fraction of the price of just a few years ago.

In addition, e-commerce creates numerous business opportunities and jobs not only in highly specialized high-tech industries, but also in vocational areas such as delivering goods that have been ordered over the Internet, or operating call centres to provide the human interface to Web buying and selling. There are also new professions, for example in the intermediation business, to provide Internet banking services, to enable grocery shopping on the Web, or brokerage activities ranging from selling stocks, cars, plane tickets, to mortgages.

This means that everybody in the developed world has the opportunity to harness the potential of e-business. But there is the big risk that even in the industrialized world physically impaired or socially disadvantaged people are left out. Nevertheless, as with developing countries, training, infrastructure access, and starting capital need to be made available. Only literate and computer-literate people can profit from e-business jobs. Basic e-business education must be offered in the elementary school. Adults also must get opportunities to acquire e-business relevant skills. This can be done by the state, but also companies should be motivated to close their labour shortages by training their own workers.* To get hands-on e-business training, but also to get access to telecommuting jobs, people need cost-efficient Internet entry. The provision of cheap and easy-to-use Internet access can be supported by the state enacting legislation that encourages competition. A deregulated telecommunication industry will strive to get access to new markets by planting more fibre cables across the whole country, offering competitively priced Internet access to everybody. Finally, investing capital to train people and to help them to use the Internet infrastructure is in the interest of the whole economy.

1.3 e-Business kills emotional intelligence?

"On the Internet, nobody knows that you are a dog!" This saying illustrates that it is extremely simple to impose on the Web whatever personality somebody desires. Communication over the Internet makes it simple to disguise any character flaws that one might have. A common view would have it that heavy Web users are frequently highly intelligent people with severe behavioural disorders. The fanatic Web user and the average computer programmer alike are considered to be nerds or geeks, with barely any social skills at all. The logical conclusions from this fact would be that to be successful on the Web and in the e-commerce economy, no social or emotional skills were needed. To be successful in the e-commerce age, one would only need good computer skills and a high IQ?

I believe that the opposite is true! I fully agree with the current emphasis on "emotional intelligence", as vividly described in the book by Daniel P. Goleman (1997). Goleman claims that not IQ, but emotional intelligence (EQ) is the strongest indicator of human success. He defines emotional intelligence to be composed of self-awareness, altruism, personal motivation, empathy, and the ability to love and be loved by friends, partners, and family members.

High emotional intelligence does not naturally correspond with high computer skills. Computer-literate people and computer experts will greatly profit from the e-business transformation – historically this has been true for

---

*In a spectacular move Ford recently announced that each one of its employees anywhere on the globe would get a subsidized high-end PC at home for $5 per month.

previous technological inventions, technically skilled people have been able to make a living off the car, from consumer electronics, or from heavy machinery during the first wave of industrialization. However, if we look at the Web services that have been the most successful to date, they are the ones working with emotions. Internet dating and matchmaking services described later in this book are typical examples of early Web successes making money from emotions, desires, and the wish to socialize with other people. Technologies like mass customization, where the computer is used to give each customer the feeling of being treated as an individual, draw on the same principles. The vendor who understands best how to rely on human emotions and desires to create his or her business will be the most successful. Advertisement, marketing, and brand-name awareness consulting companies are experiencing even higher growth than the Internet. Selling ads over the Web is one of the most profitable Internet businesses. And marketing and selling only goes by emotions!

1.4   e-Business is the death of society?

In a highly publicized study the HomeNet project (http://homenet.andrew. cmu.edu/progress/) concluded that the Internet has a negative social impact (Kraut *et al.*, 1998). The Homenet researchers monitored the well-being of a group of individuals in the Pittsburgh area. They found that the more heavily an individual used the Internet, the larger was the decline in the individual's well-being. Overall, the more time that people spent using the Internet, the more they felt depressed, lonely, and had less family communication. The most Internet-addicted users tended to communicate primarily by computer. The conclusion of the HomeNet team was that by using the Web already socially deficient people would become even lonelier.

Another issue is that privacy is potentially hard to maintain in a cyberworld. e-Business technologies allow companies to collect statistics about all aspects of our daily lives, ranging from buying patterns to where on the world we have made our phone calls at what time. Big brother has the potential to watch our actions!

Again, I have a much more positive attitude. First of all, the Homenet study has not yet been broadly verified, the sample only consisted of 169 people in 73 households, whose subjective well-being over 1 year degraded by at most one or two percentage points. It was a relatively homogeneous group not covering the whole spectrum of society and geographically confined to the greater Pittsburgh area. But more importantly, the Internet and e-business are creating new opportunities for collaboration and communication as well as numerous new virtual communities. The HomeNet study found that people had a hard time making real friends over the Internet. Among my own acquaintances, I find the Internet great for all sorts of matchmaking. It has never been easier to stay in touch with friends and colleagues around the globe. Internet technologies such as e-mail, broadcast, chat, publish and subscribe on mailing lists and in news and chat forums offer previously unheard of opportunities for asynchronous and real-time interaction. The Internet also helps to facilitate first contacts among people. The Web offers the chance to meet other people much easier than in person, or by phone. I know at least one couple that initially met on the Web in a chat room. Dating, friend-finding, and other matchmaking services are mushrooming. Virtual communities of interest in almost everything are created in daily growing numbers, ranging from recreational pastimes to professional activities. People have been starting self-help groups on the Web about rare diseases or plumbing, collecting information and providing mutual advice and support. Cyber affinity groups on how to live with diabetes, find the best mortgages, or start an anti-nuclear movement are bringing together people from diverse backgrounds and geographies but sharing common interests.

The Internet and its associated technologies make daily life easier. On-line shopping or on-line banking allow people to do necessary activities more efficiently, having more free time for recreational activities. These recreational activities can also be organized more efficiently. Background information about the next vacation trip can, for example, be collected on community Web sites about the travel destination. The actual planning of the trip and the booking of plane tickets, car rentals, and hotel reservation can then all be done much more effectively on the Web.

The Internet also makes the interaction of citizens with their government easier. The filing of taxes, the publication of community and state information, and even voting can all be done securely, privately, and more conveniently on the Web. On the other hand, legislation to safeguard privacy rights is sorely needed and is currently under way in most Western nations. Governments of the former communist East-block countries succeeded in controlling all aspects of the daily life of their citizens without using any computers. The intrusion into our privacy is much more an issue of the attitude of society towards that problem. Western countries in the USA as well as in Western Europe are very much aware of the problem, and initiatives such as the "Platform for Privacy Preferences" (P3P) of the WWW consortium define standards for the protection of an individual's privacy on the Web. Technologies for privacy protection and secure communication are readily available, it is only a question of using them!

On the individual level, e-business technologies also give handicapped and disabled people much better means to communicate and access to service, and thus assist them to lead a better life. Mute people can generate artificial sound, the deaf can recognize speech automatically, and immobilized people can get in touch with the world from their bedroom. Handicapped people can participate in the work process from home, and people in remote rural areas can participate in world trade.

In short, e-business is not a dead end for society, but it puts a unique opportunity for a better, more informed life at the fingertips of each individual!

1.5 Summary: Fundamental success factors for e-business transformation

e-Business has the potential to create a better, more liveable world. New opportunities abound. e-Business technology gives birth to new ways to cooperate and collaborate for individuals and companies alike. e-Business technology enables new modes of operation, creating numerous new business models and employment opportunities. Still, there are major obstacles to overcome. Individuals and governments need to be better aware of *legal and privacy concerns*. Success in the e-business economy requires not only IQ, but also *emotional intelligence*. It also requires that information is shared and accessible to everyone. Companies need to invest in creating a culture that *values sharing of knowledge*. Such a culture accepts change from the inside and from the outside. These companies are willing to learn from their competition, to even integrate a competitor's product and services into their own offerings to create a value-added product.

Developing countries struggling to embrace e-business teach valuable lessons to enterprises in the industrialized world. From their struggle we can distil the three e-business critical success factors:

- a differentiated approach
- continuous e-business education, and
- a collaboration infrastructure.

First of all, a *differentiated approach* based on the local environment needs to be pursued. The local environment on the macro and micro economic level matters a lot. There is no sense in using the Internet as a mass-market sales channel, if the population at large can not afford computers. On the other hand it may make sense to utilize the Internet in selected areas. While Chinese exporters for the foreseeable future will not use the Internet as main sales channel in their own country, they can very well use the Internet to sell their goods into Western countries. What is true for markets is also true for business domains. While banks are working at a furious pace to keep up with latest Internet developments, the related insurance industry has been somewhat reluctant to fully adapt the Internet sales channel or to create new service offerings based on the unique characteristics of e-business.

Secondly, continuous education and the valuation of knowledge make a big difference. The most critical success factor for Internet adaptation is education. Only computer-literate people can use the Web. Each company has to be aware of the implications of e-business for its own offerings. This awareness should exist not only on the CEO and boardroom level, but on all hierarchy levels. This implies that a company needs to *continuously train its employees in e-business related skills*.

Thirdly, companies need to invest in setting up an adequate *infrastructure for collaboration*. Any company that has more than one location must link their locations by a computer network. This used to be prohibitively expensive before the advent of the Internet. Today, using Extranet technology, even small- and medium-sized companies should not hesitate to make this investment. After having set up the physical infrastructure, a company culture that values collaboration and the sharing of knowledge is a "must have". Although setting up a successful e-business collaboration infrastructure still requires substantial up-front investment, it will pay back rapidly in improved communication and cooperation between the employees working at the different sites. This will allow companies to streamline their business processes and to create new products impossible in a company consisting of isolated islands.

Internet, e-commerce, and e-business have tremendous potential to create new business opportunities, jobs, and wealth. But it must be done right! Companies that have the information will get a competitive advantage, but companies that create a culture that values the sharing of knowledge will achieve sustainable success.

After this broad discussion of the implications of e-business for the global economy and for our society, the next chapter will now look at what a company has to do to profit from the e-business revolution.

2 *Turning business into e-business*

Introduction	Definitions of: ▶ e-Commerce ▶ e-Business ▶ Knowledge management
1 Dispelling the myths of e-business	▶ Income gaps between industrialized countries and 3rd World ▶ Re-distribution of wealth in society ▶ Isolation of individual
2 Turning business into e-business	▶ **e-Business transformation** ▶ **Business process outsourcing** ▶ **Portals** ▶ **Case study: pharmaceutical industry** ▶ **Case study: dating over the Web**
3 Blueprint for e-business implementation	▶ The information process integration blueprint ▶ e-Business deployment roadmap ▶ Knowledge management deployment ▶ e-Business project management
4 Key e-business technologies	▶ XML overview ▶ Security and digital money ▶ Virtual collaboration ▶ Workflow management ▶ Process integration by packageware
5 Tools for managing knowledge	▶ MIT process handbook ▶ Knowledge navigation

2

This chapter describes how a company can profit from the e-business revolution by transforming itself into an e-business. e-Business transformation can be done either top-down, by creating a new digital strategy, or bottom-up, by automating existing processes with e-business technologies. Either way, knowledge about its business domain and processes is one of the core assets of a company. Once process and domain knowledge has been extracted and made accessible in a human-understandable and machine-readable format, tools and technologies can link the whole value chain, automatically executing business processes spanning the globe and linking many participants. Based on a broad collection of sample processes, this chapter looks in detail at how e-business technologies can be used to transform a business either top-down or bottom-up into an e-business. A broad selection of case studies illustrates how leading firms have transformed their businesses. The Web dating industry has set an early example of a successful adaptation of all facets of Web technology.

This chapter discusses the following topics:
1. e-Business transformation
2. e-Business process outsourcing
3. Portals
4. Case study – pharmaceutical industry
5. Case study – dating over the Web

How to define new digital strategies in the e-business era is not within the scope of this book. There are other books like *Unleashing the Killer App: Digital Strategies for Market Dominance* (Downes and Mui, 1998) that give guidelines for developing strategies for the Internet world. As Downes and Mui claim

"... digital strategy is a radical new approach to strategic planning, one that doesn't pretend to create strategies so much as to create an environment where lucky foresight is more likely to make an appearance. It shares few features with traditional strategy development and deployment techniques. It values creativity and intuition. Its development is not the task of a few individuals, but of an entire organization, communicating on an as open and wide a channel as technology will permit. Most of all, it recognizes technology not as a tool for implementing a static strategy, but as a constant disrupter creating both threats and opportunities that wide-awake organizations can turn into killer apps for their own benefits."

2.1 e-Business transformation: evolution or revolution

This section will look at how technology can be used to transform an existing business into an e-business. There are five obvious reasons why it would be foolish for a company not to embrace e-business.

- *Revenue increase.* The Internet opens up a new sales channel, allowing companies to easily reach new markets that were inaccessible to them before. They also have a cost-efficient way to approach new customer segments. Mass-customization enables companies to create synergistic new product offerings based on their core competencies.
- *Cost reduction.* Many processes can be handled much more efficiently over the Web, starting from design and production, over sales and marketing, to learning and change and management and decision making. On the IT side, the open Internet standards provide an efficient means to reduce costs by reducing IT variety and complexity. Also, once a process has been adapted to operate over the Internet and the infrastructure has been set up, similar processes can be easily derived using the same infrastructure.
- *Customer retention.* The Internet has introduced concepts like mass-customization and user profiling, allowing companies to get to know their customers much better. Companies get the chance to act proactively based on previous actions of the customer and to personalize new offerings. Different sales channels can be managed in an integrated way, extending goods like plane tickets to New York with additional personalized offerings like tickets to musicals, limousine rentals, or even information about a special sale in Macy's.
- *Image improvement.* By successfully applying innovative technologies in creative ways, an enterprise gets the opportunity to establish itself as a leader among its competitors. Also, as the Internet has become an established way of communication among young and more affluent people, a company gets the chance to directly address this highly attractive customer segment.
- *Keeping up.* Today it is no longer a question of whether investing into Internet technology is a good or bad thing, but rather it must be done "because the competition is also doing it" on order to keep the options open. This allows a company to acquire know-how about Internet technologies early, and to direct investments into the areas most profitable to the core company business.

e-Business dramatically impacts almost all areas in daily business life: Companies can increase customer loyalty by offering customers a personalized way to get in touch quickly and inexpensively. Companies can reach new markets over the Internet more easily, they can create new products and services, optimize existing business processes by using leading-edge Internet technologies, they can leverage existing knowledge by making it more accessible to their employees over the Intranet, and they can better manage their risk using Web technologies for improved control and communication.

So, it is not a question of whether or not to transform a business to an e-business, but primarily of how this should be done best. Basically, there are two fundamentally different approaches and combinations that can be used.

2.1.1 Bottom-up and top-down e-business transformation

If a company wants to introduce e-business, it can choose between two different options.

- *Evolutionary process: Bottom-up.* A company can automate its existing business processes by introducing new Internet-based tools and technologies to dramatically speed up existing processes. These are processes like internal credit request, internal helpdesk automation, customer call centres, a publishing process in a workgroup, firm-wide accounting, firm-wide mail processing, procurement, or the handling of logistics.
- *Staging a revolution: Top-down.* A company can fundamentally question and rethink the business strategy and the associated business processes to make full use of the Internet and its associated technologies. Examples are the integration of the internal logistics process with an external transportation provider such as FedEx or UPS, or a pharmaceutical company might promote sales of its drugs by providing an expert system for self-medication. Or, in the tourism area, various tourism offerings could be customized and combined based on the user profile. This might also lead to the application of advanced Internet technologies to, for example, delegate search and other repetitive processes to software agents, or to automated negotiation in the areas of retail e-commerce, electricity markets, bandwidth allocation, distributed vehicle routing, or the electronic trading of financial instruments.

Both of these approaches have their merits and can be applied either exclusively or in combination. The top-down approach is suited if a company is in a business process reengineering-type of situation, where it wants to question its whole business strategy, be it as a last resort because of competitor pressure, or because a visionary management wants to explore new grounds. The bottom-up approach can be used to improve an already successful business to enlarge the lead that a company might have over its competitors.

There is now a third scenario emerging, where a company simply has to introduce e-business to catch up with its competitors. In areas like banking and finance, or global transportation, the Internet is rapidly becoming the standard way of doing business, using the Internet not only as a sales channel, but also to permanently stay in touch with the customer and to support all phases of the whole business. While it is much more straightforward to introduce e-business under these circumstances, companies choosing to be e-business followers instead of e-business leaders miss a unique opportunity to get ahead of the competition.

The underlying axiom is that e-commerce and e-business are easy, trusted, and ubiquitous. To be successful in the e-business transformation process, all issues should be approached from a multidisciplinary perspective encompassing technology, business processes and regulatory policies. Companies need to be ready to operate as virtual organizations, relying on the expertise and resources of their employees as well as their business partners.

Value should be created by bringing together vendors and end-users who possess key pieces of the Internet commerce puzzle and helping them jointly seize important market opportunities. To ensure successful integration takes a combination of vision, technology, project management, public relations, and legal advocacy.

The trend towards workflow over the Internet has led to process integration between companies as well as to process integration within the company. Workflow over the Internet makes virtual companies possible, that is companies that are put together just for the purpose of doing one job. Electronic customer care systems like Siebel and systems for automating the procurement workflow like Ariba are making it possible to automate unstructured and structured processes with prepackaged software, offering a level of convenience and thus also saving money that was unthinkable just a few years ago.

But how can a company make use of all of these new technologies, to transform itself into an e-business company. Independently of whether a company is choosing the top-down or the bottom-up approach, or a combination of both, it needs to decide on which processes to tackle first. Having an inventory of the core existing business processes is an invaluable starting point for e-business transformation. There are various ways for identifying possible candidates for process automation. Usually, a company will start with non-integrated processes that are supported by a combination of legacy applications, client/server applications, and probably some workgroup or workflow tools. The goal is to transform these processes into fully integrated processes supported by e-business applications (Fig. 2.1).

In the old IT world, there were the monolithic legacy applications, which were not integrated at all. To build more powerful applications before the advent of Internet technologies, there were two different technologies. Client/server-based applications like SAP/R3 tightly integrated different applications into one closely-knit environment based on proprietary standards. Alternatively, workgroup and workflow technologies more loosely integrated applications arranged along process boundaries. Combining these two concepts and using open Internet standards leads to fully integrated processes making extensive use of e-business technology, where applications and processes are integrated across organizational boundaries.

To identify candidate processes for bottom-up e-business transformation, we suggest ranking the candidates by the following four criteria:

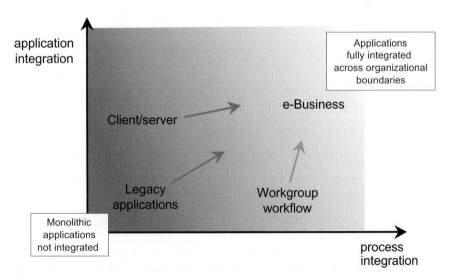

Fig. 2.1 e-Business application and process integration.

- process frequency
- process complexity
- process expansion, and
- current technology used for process automation.

Figure 2.2 illustrates the transformation criteria.

The more frequently a process is executed, i.e. the more time spent manually carrying out the work in the process, the higher the potential savings if the process is automated. e-Mail processing, call centre processing, and handling of logistics for a transportation company are processes that are executed frequently. Improving the efficiency of these processes through the use of IT can result in big potential savings in time and money.

The second criterion for a process is complexity. Simple and weakly structured processes are better supported by workgroup tools such as Lotus Notes or Microsoft Exchange, complex and highly structured processes are better implemented by workflow management systems or custom-programmed software applications.

The third criterion, expansion, is a measure for the length of the business process. Relatively short, company-internal processes can be supported by proprietary solutions and packages, or workgroup tools. Company-wide or multi-company processes spanning different regions, corporations, and countries are better supported by open Internet tools and standards.

The fourth criterion, technology, is a measure with what technology the current, not yet reengineered process is automated. Monolithic applications can be linked by workflow and middleware tools such as transaction monitors or message queuing systems. They can be made more user-friendly and easier to access by the addition of a Web browser graphical user interface (GUI). Systems built with leading-edge component technology can be linked by object

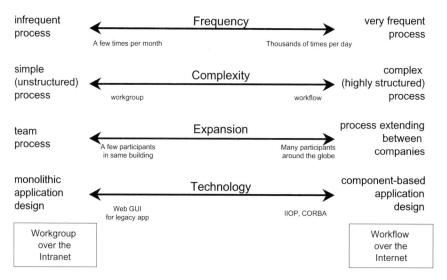

Fig. 2.2   e-Business transformation criteria.

request brokers. The technologies mentioned here are described in detail in Chapter 4.

2.1.2 e-Business evolution by example

To give an idea of how e-business technologies can be used for process automation, this section includes a listing of seven of the most common candidates for e-business process automation, assessing each candidate along the four criteria. Figure 2.3 shows the seven sample processes arranged along the two dimensions "frequency" and "complexity".

The seven samples are now discussed in detail.

2

Process Name:	*Internal credit request (e-procurement)*
Process description:	An employee sends a credit request to the group leader for approval. The approved request is then sent to the procurement department. Once the good or service has been delivered, the bill is sent to the accounting department for payment.
Technology:	This process can be easily automated using a groupware system like Lotus Notes or an e-form enabled e-mail system like Microsoft Exchange.
	On the high end, the credit request process could be reengineered as part of the overall procurement process, resulting in a top-down changed process automated with CommerceOne or Ariba (see Section 4.7.3).
Advantages:	Compared with a manually processed paper-based order form transmitted by internal mail, an electronically processed credit request can be processed much faster (hours instead of multiple days). It is much

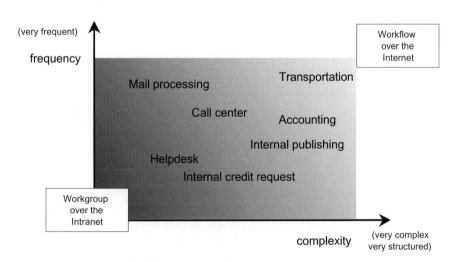

Fig. 2.3 Process frequency and complexity: from workgroup to workflow.

simpler to fill out and to send from one place to the other. The status of a pending procurement order can be easily tracked.

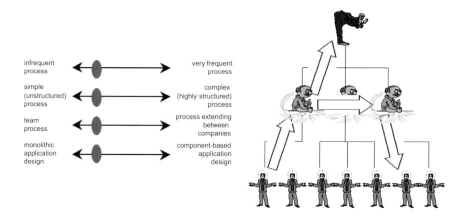

infrequent process	←●→	very frequent process
simple (unstructured) process	←●→	complex (highly structured) process
team process	←●→	process extending between companies
monolithic application design	←●→	component-based application design

Process Name:	*Helpdesk in large corporation*
Process description:	An employee sends a request for assistance to the first-level-support staff. First-level-support opens a new incident in the systems. If the problem cannot be solved, it is forwarded to the second-level-support staff. If the problem can still not be solved, it is forwarded to the producer. Escalation levels in the helpdesk support systems are freely definable. Parameters such as the number of support levels, people at the helpdesk, access rights to the helpdesk, etc. can be flexibly configured. Incidents can be attached for processing to a single person or a group.
Technology:	Helpdesks can be flexibly automated by a groupware system. There are also custom-built off-the-shelf help-desk packages available, offering a GUI (graphical user interface) for the handling of the incidents, a knowledge base for collecting and archiving the solved incidents, integration into the e-mail system, etc.
Advantages:	An IT-based helpdesk system requires defined procedures and defined response times. It is possible to introduce service-dependent billing. The status of each incident can be checked. If the organization changes, helpdesk flow can be easily adapted. The unified user interface enables simple direct access to case information for end users and helpdesk staff.

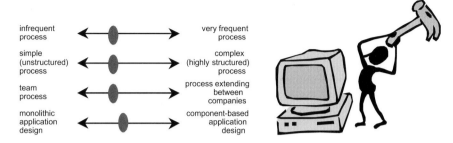

Process Name: *Customer call centre*

Process description: The call centre agents accept calls and enter the incidents into the IT system. If needed, an agent then triggers the redirection to a case worker. Success control and feedback can be automatically collected by the system, and information about each case is readily available.

Technology: For a larger call centre, a dedicated call centre tool such as Vantive or Siebel (see Section 4.7.4) is usually used, including computer integrated telephony functionality. For a small call centre, a workgroup tool can be used.

Advantages: Statistics such as the number of calls per time unit, per employee, per group, per time of day, per customer type, etc. can be automatically collected. The status of each incident can be checked. Software applications can be directly linked to the incident, resulting in improved throughput and much higher service quality.

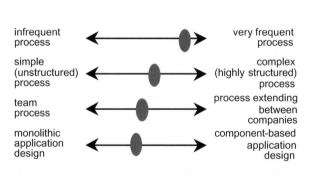

Process Name: *Publishing process*

Process description: Formal documentation in large organizations is frequently authored and controlled by teams of authors and editors. Current-generation text processing tools are integrated with document management and groupware systems. After the initial authoring phase, a draft document is transferred to a workflow system with

	defined work steps and reaction times up to the publication.
Technology:	Text processing with versioning functions, document management with multiple author and archival functions, groupware systems for the definition and processing of the workflow.
Advantages:	Improved support of the creation process results in free authoring and well-structured post-processing. The authoring process can follow well-defined organizational rules. The entire process can be handled using one integrated platform.

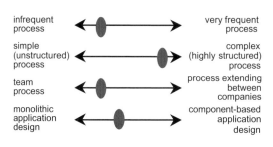

Process Name:	*Customization of firm-wide accounting*
Process description:	Accounting is usually implemented in large companies using ERP packages such as SAP, Peoplesoft, Baan, or Oracle. While these packages excel in areas of predefined functionality, they rarely cover all the needs of the company. Accounting procedures are normally implemented in the accounting standard software package. Customized functions such as marketing tasks, the creation of mass mailings from databases, the routing of documents to external parties, etc. can be added by document management and groupware systems.
Technology:	Business processes are defined with the "package-internal" technologies such as SAP Workflow. Extensions are added by Internet-based groupware and document management systems.
Advantages:	Long and complex processes are supported by pre-defined and hard-to-modify off-the-shelf accounting packages. Small, customized tasks can be quickly, flexibly, and cheaply added with groupware systems.

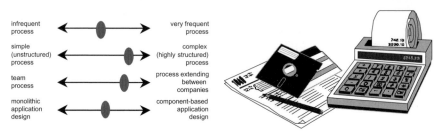

2

infrequent process	←——●——→	very frequent process
simple (unstructured) process	←——●——→	complex (highly structured) process
team process	←——●——→	process extending between companies
monolithic application design	←——●——→	component-based application design

Process Name: *Firm-wide mail processing*

Process description: Despite all the promises of the so-called paperless offices, companies are still flooded with incoming paper mail. Electronic processing of correspondence in a company with offices at different locations makes this correspondence universally accessible. This problem is frequently addressed by implementing centralized mail input and scanning facilities. The scanned-in documents are then distributed to caseworkers, which, in turn, can trigger the appropriate actions.

Technology: This application combines document management, workgroup, workflow and archival systems. The workflow can be supported on the Intranet by using an Internet-based groupware or workflow system. Access can be simplified by a unified HTML-GUI displaying scanned-in documents, work lists and forms. "Classical" client/server-applications can transparently be linked into the process in the background.

Advantages: The documents are accessible from anywhere at any time. The GUI is independent of products, which makes the whole system easier to maintain, modify, and extend.

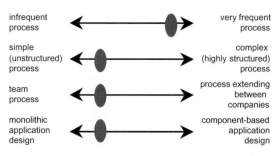

infrequent process	←————●————→	very frequent process
simple (unstructured) process	←————●————→	complex (highly structured) process
team process	←————●————→	process extending between companies
monolithic application design	←————●————→	component-based application design

Process Name: *Logistics on-line tracking of shipped goods*

Process description: Transportation providers like UPS or FedEx assume full responsibility for the entire transportation process. Their client companies can link their order handling and accounting systems with the UPS or FedEx shipping system. This allows customers to immediately get access to the shipping status of their orders. Individual FedEx or UPS customers can also start and

	track their shipping over the Web, printing their own mailing labels, and arrange for pickup and delivery.
Technology:	UPS and FedEx integrate their shipping and billing applications with Web access for clients, providing a set of applications for corporate customers as well as a Web GUI for individual clients.
Advantages:	Customers have access to "their" process. The location of a mailing is traceable anytime. Corporate users can outsource a peripheral function to a specialized service provider, tightly integrated with their own business process.

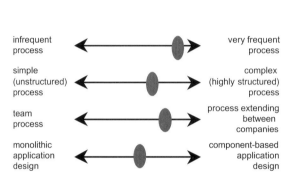
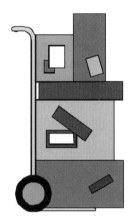

2.1.3 e-Business transformation principles

As the samples from above have shown, Internet technology offers radically new opportunities: Information is now accessible from anywhere on the globe. People can communicate instantaneously regardless of location. Markets are global in a scale that has never been possible before. Companies can tap into global supplier networks to get the best resources for their needs from anywhere on the globe.

Mass customization allows companies to easily offer personalized goods to anybody on the globe with Internet access. The seamless integration of different media types and the unified Web user interface to all sorts of applications and data affords the creation of new products and services consisting of combinations that were previously impossible. Existing products, services, and information can be packaged into new products, combining goods and information while keeping the knowledge of the fundamental processes as the core asset of the company.

Based on these principles companies need to adapt, modify, or radically change their business model. Under the term business model, I understand

(1) what a company does, and
(2) how it makes money from doing it.

Professor Tom Malone from the MIT Sloan School of Business distinguishes four fundamentally different types of business models for e-business companies:

- *Creators*: These can be producers of physical goods such as Dell or Compaq, but also producers of information such as the on-line version of the *Wall Street Journal*.
- *Distributors*: These are companies like Amazon, or Barnes & Noble.
- *Brokers*: These are companies like on-line auctioneer eBay, on-line travel agent Travelocity, or on-line group buying agency Accompany.
- *Extractors*: These are the "true" Web portal companies like Yahoo, Lycos, or Alta Vista whose business model is based on advertising revenue. To improve advertising revenue, they need to get as many user site visits as possible.

The basic implementation procedure to put e-business in place is rather straightforward and applicable for any business that wants to engage in e-business transformation:

(1) Extend own products by integrating competing products into own offerings, using imagination, creativity, human desires, and emotion.
(2) Build a rapid prototype using advanced Web technologies.
(3) Test the idea quickly in real life.
(4) Continuously refine and/or redo from scratch.

As an inspiration and for implementation, a combination of the new and creative business ideas and the generic best practice processes should be used. The best practice processes can, for example, come from the Process Handbook repository (Fig. 2.4) which is described in Chapter 5.

There are a few guiding principles to successfully transform a business to e-business that need to be kept in mind.

1. Transformation principle: Think global, act local

While information, goods, and people can be accessed anywhere on the globe, the only thing that is truly globally accessible is information. While a business can be run anywhere on the globe, access to transportation is crucial for shipping physical goods. Virtual companies have not yet taken off to the extent envisioned by Internet enthusiasts. In spite of teleworking, e-mail, groupware, and virtual reality, it is still the human contact that counts. Nevertheless, the globally networked corporate environment allows companies to split up processes much more flexibly and adjust to the physical availability of the workers. Manual labour performed half a world away by an unskilled workforce can be linked with high-tech work done by the white-collar worker

Business idea (value proposition) ⎫
                                   ⎬ Transformed
Generic best-practice process (process handbook) ⎭ e-Business process

Figure 2.4 e-Business transformation.

in the industrialized world. The Web also supports continuous education and training of the workers anywhere in the world. The Internet can be used around the globe for business-to-business communication between suppliers, producers, and customers, particularly for multinational corporations and large SMEs (small- and medium-sized enterprises). On the other hand, Internet access to the mass market is still limited to the USA, Western Europe, Japan, Australia, and Singapore.

2. Transformation principle: Give away information

It is very hard for potential buyers of "information" to assess the quality of this good as a commodity. The only way to convince customers is to give away free samples. Vendors of stock quotes give away time-deferred quotes, while buyers pay good money for real-time quotes. In return for free information, potential buyers return their own interest profiles to allow vendors to customize their offerings to their needs (mass customization). Giving away information for free also allows the vendor to distinguish itself from the competition. In addition, customers getting information for free are willing to accept lower quality and to give corrective feedback to the information providers, who in return, can improve their offerings. Particularly in highly competitive industries, there is no way around providing added value to the main good sold to attract potential buyers. User profiling pioneer firefly.com added ratings of other listeners to the music CDs they were selling, allowing potential customers to select CDs they might like based on the tastes of other listeners. A generalization of this idea is to use search engines to provide uniform information access to their own and competitor information. Educated potential customers will use search engines anyway to compare a company's product with the products of the competitor. This will enable a company to become the entry point, or portal, to a certain subject area.

3. Transformation principle: Virtualization

The Internet supports collaborative processes on a global scale. Groupware, teleconferencing, and other related technologies enable new forms of cooperation. Nevertheless, people still trust other people better than computers, and to get cooperation started and mutual trust established there is no replacement for face-to-face meetings. In principle, though, Internet-only companies like Amazon.com, or eBay operate primarily as a virtual operation, leveraging an existing infrastructure of book warehouses or linking a huge network of single item vendors and bidders. Going to market over the Web exclusively does not mean that there is no real distribution system needed. In the case of Amazon, customers expect reliable, cost-efficient, and most importantly, speedy delivery of books and other goods. To improve control over its distribution system, Amazon has been recently forced to buy an established book wholesaler with widespread physical warehouses and distribution facilities.

Virtualization means that any company that wants to transform its business to e-business needs to find ways to virtualize its business, by, for example, reaching new customer segments over the Web or changing its business model to partner with other companies to offer new products. For large monolithic enterprises this means that they have to break themselves up into pieces and operate as a virtual network of companies. For example, a manufacturing company can split its supply chain into smaller independent companies, and then outsource the old functions to these new and nimble companies, while only the core competency remains with the original enterprise. To react quickly to change, a new business process must be createable instantaneously; this is much easier to achieve for a network of small companies than for one large monolithic organization. In short, virtualization provides for organic forms, improvisation, individual responsibility, and for fast reactions to change.

4. Transformation principle: Conventional wisdom still counts

Over the last few years the excitement and hype of Internet enthusiasm have led journalists and industry experts to challenge fundamental business principles (Gallaugher, 1999). It was assumed that *brand strength* would not matter so much for Web companies, that small and innovative companies would get customers based on the quality of their offerings. Experience has shown that the opposite is true, that customers tend to flock to the Web sites of well-established players in the real world, neglecting small high-quality startups. Drawing consumers to an unseen storefront is a challenging and expensive venture. At one time, Amazon was spending roughly $36 in marketing for every $100 in sales.

It was suggested that on-line firms would face less pressure to grow and achieve *economies of scale*. However, on-line brokers like E*TRADE can offer competitive on-line prices because of their large trading volume. Offering clients a huge inventory of goods is one of the biggest advantages of the Web. However, offering a large inventory is the easier if a company has already a large inventory in their physical stores. Although everybody can open an Internet mall on a PC, size still remains critically important to success on the Web. Economies of scale, brand awareness and the wish of consumers to join Web communities with the largest number of users all favour *size* and rapid growth. Consumers have to invest in learning to use a particular Web site. They want to minimize that investment by getting as few Web sites as possible to cover as many needs as possible.

The Web was also touted as the death of the middlemen. Disintermediation would bring extinction to travel services, bookstores, and other middlemen. Reality has shown otherwise: Amazon, eBay, CD-Now, and E*TRADE can all be thought of as middlemen, selling the products of others. What happens is that weak points in the value chain are replaced by technology-driven enhancements. On-line car dealers bring together buyers and sellers of used cars much more efficiently that the old style used-car salesmen. Order-taking delivery staff, which is not needed anymore in the age of Web ordering, can now, for example, provide added value by offering home delivery.

But still the most important factor is timing. Failures of innovative products that were ahead of their time abound: the videophone and early Internet magazines like Hotwired are just a few examples of failures. Nevertheless, early movers can experiment, defining the market and experiencing exponential growth, while latecomers have to compensate by investing heavily in marketing and application development to catch up to the early movers. The failure of Barnes & Noble to catch up to Amazon delivers a compelling example!

2.1.4 Enabling technologies for transformation

The information technologies listed in Chapter 4 provide the technical foundation for e-business transformation. Technologies for manipulating and locating information are absolutely crucial to provide added value to existing products. *Information filtering* is one key technology, employing methods such as collaborative filtering, where users can search for information based on other user's experiences and preferences. Constraint-based filtering restricts searches based on external constraints. Rule-based filtering uses artificial intelligence techniques to optimize searches based on domain-specific rules. Information filtering can then be applied by offering potential customers search engines to render uniform information access to both their own and competitors' information, thus providing added value and becoming the Web access point of choice for a specific subject.

Another core Web technology is *user profiling*. Collecting information about preferences of the users allows vendors to adapt their offerings to the needs and tastes of their customers. They can then target their marketing efforts much more efficiently, offering each customer what she or he is looking for. Vendors can also customize their products, creating new products that would not be possible without collecting user profiling information, for example selling mass-tailored clothing or computers assembled to the needs and tastes of each customer.

In the future *agent* concepts will also gain great importance. Users will delegate searching and other repetitive tasks to agents. Companies that offer agent-based services will gain a competitive advantage. Typical applications are in the areas of automated negotiation for goods, in retail e-commerce, in electricity markets to shop for electricity, in bandwidth allocation in phone and computer networks, in distributed vehicle routing in logistics applications, and in the electronic trading of financial instruments.

2.1.5 e-Business Transformation Inspirations

To illustrate how e-business has the potential to transform the way in which business is conducted, we will now look at some innovative ideas covering different business domains.

Drug manufacturing

The obvious idea is to use the Internet as a sales channel to sell drugs over the Web. To make full use of the two-way communication capabilities of the Web, the manufacturer could, for example, provide analysis tools for the self-medication of non-prescription drugs, allowing clients to identify the best drug for their sickness. If the manufacturer wanted to offer added value to its clients, it could complement the database of its own drugs with a full listing of drugs from other manufacturers to implement a complete expert system for the analysis and cure of common light illnesses (www.pharmweb.net).

Chinese gift importer

A company that wanted to import gifts from China could use the Internet as the main sales channel to sell gifts directly to US consumers over the Web. The key is to have a value-added offering, by, for example, integrating gifts of other vendors on its own Web site. Adding cultural background information about each gift could further enrich the contents of the Web site. Chinese history experts could, for example, write these descriptions. The Web site could be made even more attractive to users by adding a search engine that would filter out the ideal gift based on individual user profiles (http://www.chinamalls. com/).

Pajama vendor

The pajama vendor could enable the customers on its Web site to custom-tailor their pajamas by, for example, choosing their desired cut and cloth pattern (http://www.landsend.com/cd/frontdoor/).

Internet banking

The Internet bank could offer an integrated financial package, containing checking account, mutual funds, shares and options, and mortgages, combined with Web pay presentment and payment, all flexibly linked, to offer the customer maximum transparency. Background information for all financial products offered can be easily included on the Web site. The Internet bank can also put together more comprehensive packages by integrating competing offerings as extensions into its own package (http://ganges.cs.tcd.ie/mepeirce/ Project/oninternet.html).

Tourism provider

Individual tourism providers and tourist chambers of commerce could set up Web sites offering mass customization of individual customers based on their user profiles. They could integrate their own offerings with vendors of other services such as banking, gift shops, etc. Local specialist tourist vendors could also team up with global tourism vendors such as travelocity.com or lowestfare.com to draw more tourists to their specialist offerings (http:// www.nytoday.com/).

These are just a few simple examples to give a faint glimpse on what businesses are doing today to harness the potential of e-business. Finally, it will depend on the creativity and the willingness to break new grounds of each individual enterprise, to become the leader in its field, or even to venture out into unknown grounds and define a new business field of its own.

2.2 Business process outsourcing over the Web

Once business processes have been reengineered to fit the e-business environment, they need to be implemented. Ideally, this implementation should be as painless for the company as possible. It should be automatic, rapid, and inexpensive. This is very hard to achieve, particularly for software projects. And implementing a new e-business process usually means putting new software into place! Although software vendors promise that it has never been easier to install and configure their packaged, component-built applications, reality is otherwise. The growing functionality of new software continuously branching out into new application domains has made software deployment increasingly complex. Even a modestly large software system is impossible to install without a major investment in time, money, and external consultants. Companies increasingly try to avoid this hassle by moving the operations of whole business processes to external outsourcing companies. This fits well with the current tendency to focus on core competencies and have all the non-crucial services performed and managed by outside service providers.

Business process outsourcing is the long-term contracting of a company's business processes to an outside service provider. Companies are outsourcing business processes to outside service providers in the hope of getting the same service at a lower cost and better quality. This should allow the company's management to focus its attention full-time on the company's core business. In the 1950s, there were the fully integrated companies that were doing everything internally. Since then, more and more of the non-critical business functions have been moved to external service providers. This started with peripheral functions like security services or janitorial and housecleaning services.

In the meantime, large professional services firms like Deloitte Consulting or PricewaterhouseCoopers are providing a full range of outsourcing services. The following list of outsourcing areas is by no means conclusive:

- Finance and accounting – Management of financial and accounting department functions to streamline planning, controls, and processing.
- Internal audit – Management of business, operating, and financial risks and ongoing evaluation and strengthening of internal accounting controls.
- Tax compliance – Management of home country and international tax return planning and preparation to reduce taxes and processing costs.
- Procurement – Management of strategic procurement and global sourcing to optimize savings and profitability.
- Human resources – Management of cost-competitive HR programs designed to attract, retain, and motivate workers.
- Real estate management – Management of facilities to improve real estate operations, property usage, asset management, and administration.
- Applications process – Management of enterprise resource planning systems and individual software applications that support business processes.

Business process outsourcing means moving the entire business functions to the outsourcing provider, who then assumes full responsibility for processing these functions. To successfully outsource parts of a business, the business needs to be split into disjoined vertical pieces where each piece is made up of an entire business process.

The Internet has enabled a new brand of outsourcing, where the outsourcing provider is linked directly to core processes of the company. Rather than vertically splitting the business by moving whole processes such as the recruiting process to the outsourcing provider, business processes can be cut

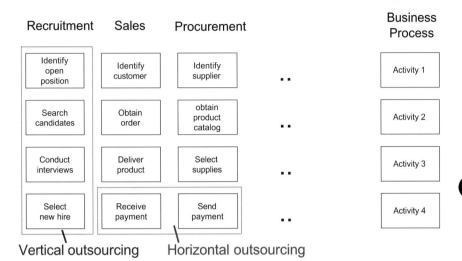

Recruitment   Sales   Procurement   Business Process

Identify open position	Identify customer	Identify supplier	..	Activity 1
Search candidates	Obtain order	obtain product catalog	..	Activity 2
Conduct interviews	Deliver product	Select supplies	..	Activity 3
Select new hire	Receive payment	Send payment	..	Activity 4

Vertical outsourcing   Horizontal outsourcing

Fig. 2.5   Vertical and horizontal business process outsourcing.

into horizontal pieces, where different parties can operate different parts of the process (Fig. 2.5). Examples of this sort of outsourcing are operations of business travel, handling of the logistics process, procurement, or customer billing.

A closer look at the four generic process groups (Fig. 2.6) reveals that the groups have reached different levels of outsourcing maturity. Well-structured processes such as "buying and selling" and "design and production" are well suited to business process outsourcing, while unstructured processes like

Buying and selling	structured	Customer relationship management	Vertical & Horizontal BPO
Design and production	structured	Enterprise resource planning	Vertical & Horizontal BPO
Learning and change	unstructured	Knowledge navigation	Horizontal Web
Management and decision making	unstructured	MIS data-warehousing	Horizontal Web
	Organization and industry structures	IT Technology	Outsourcing

Fig. 2.6   Four main generic process categories.

"learning and change" or "management and decision making" are candidates for horizontal Web outsourcing.

2.2.1 Business travel outsourcing

Large companies usually have their own internal travel departments which handle all the business travel needs of the employees of the company. They justify their existence by two arguments: first, they make it more convenient for employees to plan their travel because they do not have to deal with plane schedules and fares, hotel reservations, and rental car companies. Second, corporate travel officials are able to cut better deals with travel agencies, airline companies, hotel chains, and rental car companies, using their corporate bargaining power.

Recently, Internet-based travel agencies have emerged, moving into the realms of internal business travel departments. They offer the same advantages as internal travel departments, namely convenient booking, and corporate rates, albeit at much lower cost, namely close to zero. Also, they can offer the same services not only to large companies, but also to small- and medium-sized enterprises.

Travel services come in two varieties. Similar to the travel Web sites that cater to the need of individual and recreational tourists, there are now also travel Web sites for business travellers. Biztravel.com is offering a full range of services, integrating plane tickets, hotels, and car rentals with other business travel needs such as reservation of meeting facilities, or support for the organization of a seminar. And everything that can be done fully automatically over the Internet cuts out the corporate travel office! The QualityAgent travel management software booking tool (www.wwts.com/QualityAgent.html) goes one step further by putting a specialized Web-enabled corporate travel application on the desktop of all employees of QualityAgent customer companies. The QualityAgent software also incorporates corporate travel policy parameters.

2.2.2 Logistics outsourcing

Shipping companies UPS and FedEx have been early adopters of the Web, adding a Web interface to their logistics applications. The Web interface enabled customers to track their parcels on the road, providing them with new capabilities that were previously unheard of, while at the same time relieving FedEx and UPS customer representatives from having to answer these inquiries by phone. Today, the global shipping companies have gone much further; putting the full interface to all shipping-related functions into the hands of their clients. For example, customers print their own shipping labels on-line both with UPS and FedEx. But integration of business processes goes much further. FedEx offers a complete suite of software products, starting from the casual shipper up to large corporations shipping hundreds of parcels every day. These software tools not only automate the shipping process, but also directly link into the processes of FedEx customers. They provide links into accounting, generate condensed expense reports, and they automatically initiate customs clearance for shipping into foreign countries. FedEx even

offers supply chain management tools for warehousing, inventory control and
the processing of returns of shipped mailings.

2.2.3 Procurement outsourcing

Tools from vendors like Ariba or CommerceOne enable a company to entirely
outsource procurement over the Web. Before the Web, there used to be an
internal procurement department responsible for all aspects of stocking the
company office supplies, negotiating the best deals with suppliers, defining
corporate policies for buying office furniture, photocopiers, etc. Putting an
Ariba supply-ordering applet on the desk of every employee cuts out the
procurement department. Corporate buying policies can now be automated by
using Internet procurement marketplaces like ariba.com. Companies can now
automatically keep track of the supplies that their employees need. They can
decide on whether they want to give employees freedom to choose on the
Internet marketplace the cheapest or best product, or whether they want to
enforce corporate buying policies by restricting access to the offerings of
approved vendors, while at the same time collecting all the statistics they want.

2.2.4 Payment outsourcing

There are now companies like Yahoo and CheckFree's Bill Pay, Microsoft's
Transpoint, or Swiss PayNet offering integrated Internet payment services,
cutting out intermediaries like banks, post offices, or cheque-clearing centres.
While Bill Pay and Transpoint primarily address individuals, companies can
outsource all or part of their billing and payment process to PayNet. A
company transmits information about goods or services delivered to its clients
to PayNet; PayNet takes care of sending an electronic bill to the customer,
which can then automatically authorize payment by one mouse click. After the

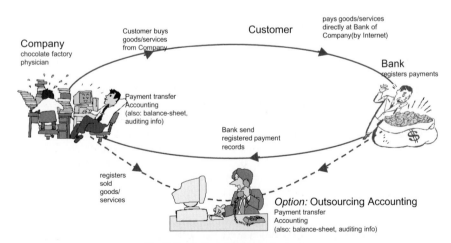

Fig. 2.7 Outsourced payment process.

customer authorizes payment, the money is automatically transferred to the account of the company.

PayNet offers various combinations of paper-based and Internet-based billing, starting at the low end by getting listing of clients, and mailing them paper bills for payment. This functionality can be naturally extended to combine electronic payment outsourcing with accounting outsourcing. PayNet links with packages that have accounting functions like SAP or Peoplesoft, to get transaction records directly into the accounting system. This allows companies, for example, to automatically collect balance sheet and audit information.

2.2.5 Web hosting of Internet malls

Internet access providers are increasingly offering business process out-sourcing services. They started by selling networking bandwidth, later Web hosting services were added, storing other companies' Web pages on the access provider's Web servers. IBM and AT&T, among others, are now offering integrated e-commerce services, setting up and operating other companies' Internet malls on their own servers, linking into the customer's ERP systems. HP's e-vis.com (http://www.e-vis.com/) is typical of the latest generation of outsourced Web hosting service provider, extending a second-generation on-line marketplace by offering clients the ability to add their own users on-line and to acquire enhanced functionality by simply downloading additional components. In addition, e-vis.com also includes the ability for distributed project groups to share documents and data, identify issues and work as a team. Project decisions and the decision-making process are captured by e-vis.com in real-time by providing conference capabilities, enabling real-time collaboration between project team members. It offers search and change notification tools such that team members can stay abreast of changing information, having access to the latest news and to an interactive on-line training centre.

2.2.6 Common characteristics for horizontal outsourcing

Travel, logistics, procurement, and payment outsourcing have some common characteristics. They are all "horizontal" processes, providing building blocks for vertical "business critical" processes. They cover non-business critical functions, where the primary goal for process improvement for a company is to save money, instead of generating new business. In all of these horizontal activities, company-internal support functions are made superfluous by directly linking internal users over the internet to the external service provider, for example Internet travel agents, shipping companies, Internet procurement mall operators, and electronic payment providers. These internal users are employees that have been users of the services of the internal travel department, the procurement department, or the billing department. Horizontal outsourcing cuts out intermediaries, the value-add of intermediaries is offered by Internet-based software in combination with outsourcing companies offering services that would be unthinkable without the Internet. The service offered over the Internet is cheaper, faster, and more reliable than with conventional means. An external service provider like an Internet travel agent is able to deliver a higher quality service than its internal counterpart, because of the higher transaction volume and because of its amassed experience which is the result of specialization on a task which is not business-critical for its client companies.

Other examples abound: Sun and Microsoft both plan to offer text-processing applications over the Internet. As so-called application service providers (ASP), they join large computer manufacturers like HP or IBM that plan to provide application software by charging by the hour for access to services. In the future these ASP companies could make the computer industry resemble the electricity industry as it stands now, where the HP's and IBM's will be the equivalent of the power generating companies, while their smaller ASP competitors will be the equivalent of the local power distributors.

2

2.2.7 Enabling technologies for outsourcing

Internet technologies offer the ideal environment for business process outsourcing. The Web provides open standardized information access, seamlessly linking a company and its outsourcing provider. Virtual collaboration tools like groupware or teleconferencing allow teams with members from different companies to communicate easily. Virtual malls give a company the opportunity to entirely outsource the sales process. The standardization of general business process automation on a few systems from dominant vendors like SAP, Siebel, or Ariba forces companies to adapt their processes to work with these packages. This makes life easier for outsourcing providers, because they can set up large computing centres running multiple versions of these packages for multiple customers. While large outsourcing clients still might have their own SAP installation operated by the outsourcing company, small- and medium-sized companies can share applications by each having a different instance of the same application running on a shared server.

2.3   From Web sites to portals

e-Commerce, buying and selling over the Internet, has been seen as the dominant use of the Web since its inception. In the meantime e-business has evolved as the enabler for re-engineering the whole value network of a company, far surpassing the initial scope of e-commerce. Nevertheless, the end user predominantly judges the e-business quality of a company by the quality of the company's Web site. In the race to come up with ever better Web sites attracting more customers, Web sites have evolved into portals.

A portal is a Web site that proposes to be a major starting site for users when they get connected to the Web or that users tend to visit as an anchor site. To fulfil this requirement, a portal combines different characteristics. A portal is an entry point to the Web. It is also an integration platform for applications and information on the Web, as well as a personalized electronic workplace. The goal is to become a growing, highly dynamic attraction point for communities. Finally, a portal also wants to act as an information distributor, decreasing transaction costs for its owners and users.

There are two types of portals: horizontal portals and vertical portals. Horizontal portals provide search functions and classification for the whole Web content as well as general Web functionality, such as email, discussion groups, or personalized pages. Horizontal portals attempt to serve the entire Internet community. Their critical success factor usually is the use of superior Web technology. Trying to establish a horizontal portal is in the realm of the "classical" Internet startups. Typical examples of horizontal portals are Yahoo or Lycos.

Vertical portals provide the same functions as horizontal portals, but are focussed on a specific industry or community. A special instance of a vertical portal is the corporate portal. A corporate portal is intended to become the electronic workplace of choice for the workers of a company, integrating in-house and external applications and information. Vertical portals target a niche audience on the Internet. The critical success factor for a vertical portal is industrial competence and a strong brand. Vertical portals are usually started by well-established non-Internet companies attempting to establish a portal for their industry segment. Successful examples of vertical corporate portals are the Dell or Cisco portals (Fig. 2.8).

There are many reasons why a company would want to establish a corporate portal. A well-established portal is a strong argument for a company to claim thought-leadership in its area. On the practical side, a strong portal will bring a majority of relevant visits to its site, which will result in more advertising and e-commerce revenue. On its own portal, a company can expect enhanced sales of its own products and services, since they can get preferential treatment on the portal. A portal can also bring preferred relationships with enterprises related to its market.

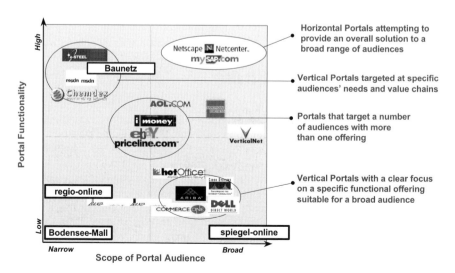

Fig. 2.8 Horizontal and vertical portals (source: Deloitte Consulting).

A company has three options to participate in the booming portal business:

- establish a self-sufficient portal
- participate in an established portal, or
- raise awareness by being listed at top positions of search output on Web search engines.

If a company decides to build its own portal, it must be willing to cover high initial investment costs. On its portal, it must provide superficial, as well as community-specific content. It also should offer free user services, such as email accounts, personalization and user home pages, and ISP (Internet service provider) services. In addition, contents must be localized. The goal has to be to offer real added value to the user community that the company wants to attract, which includes many services which do not directly support sales of the company's product.

There are different business models for a company to generate sustainable income. Is the goal of the portal:

- to generate short-term revenue?
- to maintain and increase market share?
- to reduce costs? or
- to provide access to a new sales channel?

Depending on the planned goal, revenue generation can then be based on:

- an advertising model
- selling subscriptions for premium content
- charging transaction fees
- collecting commissions on other people's sales, or
- finding sponsorships for the portal.

A company can also decide to pursue a more modest approach by becoming a member in an established portal. In this case it should partner with a portal that carries a strong brand in the same area (Fig. 2.9). This is mostly of interest to enterprises that have compelling content – of general, location, or community-specific interest. The key is to brand the company's content within the context of a larger portal brand, with the goal of not just adding to

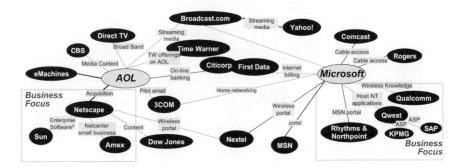

Fig. 2.9   Portal alliance strategy of Microsoft and AOL.

the portal's content offering, but to be recognized as a valuable contributor on its own.

If a company does not want to invest into a portal itself, it should at least leverage its Internet presence by trying to become a dominant contender for search result output. This means that if users search for a topic relevant to the company, the company's Web pages should be at the top of the search results returned by the search engine. Most enterprises will find themselves in this category, seeking neither to become a portal, nor a portal member. The techniques to reach that goal are two-fold. First, the Web pages need to incorporate accurate metadata for the search engines. Secondly, the Web site should be advertised at other locations, be it on the Web, or using other media.

Whether a company wants to establish an internal corporate portal, or to set up an external vertical portal, there is a long list of different requirements that must be considered. The portal should contain the corporate taxonomy, to define a common language. Search and access functions to internal information need to be provided, as well as the capabilities to search and access external business data sources. The corporate portal can be used to access management information and to support knowledge management. Information about partners, competitors, associations, and other Internet portals must be made available. e-Mail, calendaring, and collaboration tools should be integrated into the portal. In the case of an internal corporate portal it should be possible to access and integrate enterprise applications over the portal. Personalization features as well as adequate security mechanisms should be offered. The portal can also be used as a "social vehicle", by integrating blackboard, news, personal home pages, and announcements. Figure 2.10 lists the full requirements for building a successful portal, grouped into five focus areas.

As language, culture and various levels of development divide the European market, it will be difficult to create pan-European portals. Many European content ventures have adopted a portal business model for their national market. While there will be space for smaller, local, portals on the national level, some of Europe's existing portals will consolidate into a few multi-national portals.

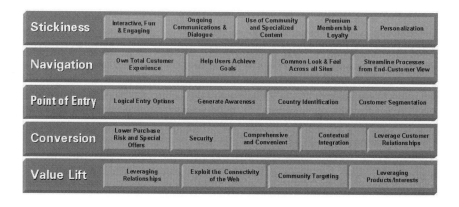

Stickiness	Interactive, Fun & Engaging	Ongoing Communications & Dialogue	Use of Community and Specialized Content	Premium Membership & Loyalty	Personalization
Navigation	Own Total Customer Experience	Help Users Achieve Goals	Common Look & Feel Across all Sites	Streamline Processes from End-Customer View	
Point of Entry	Logical Entry Options	Generate Awareness	Country Identification	Customer Segmentation	
Conversion	Lower Purchase Risk and Special Offers	Security	Comprehensive and Convenient	Contextual Integration	Leverage Customer Relationships
Value Lift	Leveraging Relationships	Exploit the Connectivity of the Web	Community Targeting	Leveraging Products/Interests	

Fig. 2.10 Five focus areas of successful portals (source: Deloitte Consulting).

The vertical portal concept is of great importance for the e-business economy. e-Commerce and customer support are converging, offering customized services to potential and existing customers alike. New entrants in this market have a chance to become leading players by establishing a strong portal brand without setting up an actual physical presence.

Sections 2.4 and 2.5 discuss two case studies where portals have been used successfully. In the first case study, we will look, among others, at a corporate portal for a leading pharmaceutical company. As a second case study, we will look at the Web dating industry, which has been using the portal concept highly successfully before even the name of Web portal was known.

2

2.4 Case study: pharmaceutical industry

To illustrate the generic e-business transformation process, this section introduces some real case studies. In the first case study I will describe selected projects from my own consulting work. These projects have been completed for various clients mostly in the pharmaceutical industry in the past 3 years. The clients are large multinational corporations that have subsidiaries around the globe. Taken together, the projects illustrate the full e-business transformation process. The sample projects are grouped according to the Information Process Integration (IPI) Blueprint described in the next chapter.

The first level of e-business transformation according to the IPI-Blueprint is the transformation of *information*. The information transformation case study describes how we set up a corporate portal to manage the knowledge in a large pharmaceutical company. The second level of the IPI-Blueprint deals with the automation of company-internal business *processes*. As an example, the development of a groupware system to support information sharing and collaboration among field engineers working around the globe is described. A second process example discusses the implementation of a workflow based system to support the core business processes of a financial services company. The third IPI level includes the full *integration* of the value chain. As an example the Internet-based integration of the supply chain of pharmaceutical companies is discussed.

2.4.1 Intranet-based knowledge management by a corporate portal

A large multinational pharmaceutical company wanted us to set up an Internet-based infrastructure for the management of their domain knowledge. Our intent was to produce a comprehensive Web-based information environment by developing a distribution infrastructure for company-internal information sources. Towards that goal we had to create a secure environment for the distribution of information across the Intranet. The intent of the management of our client was to encourage a culture of information sharing within the context of projects, tasks, functions, and organizational groups and roles. On the technical level, this meant to integrate diverse information sources such as shared file systems, e-mail, and document and data repositories.

We split the whole project into sub-projects as shown in Fig. 2.11.

First we set up the Web infrastructure, by installing the Web servers, and defining operations procedures resolving issues like Web server naming conventions. We also had to set up a company-wide user directory, which is a non-trivial task for thousands of users who are spread out around the globe. We solved this problem by decentralizing the responsibility for the directory maintenance. We also had to define security and access policies, for example setting clear rules for dial-in access from outside of the corporate Intranet.

The authoring-related sub-projects delivered tools and guidelines support-ing the content providers of the Intranet. As the goal was to encourage sharing of information, we wanted to make it as simple as possible to post information. Nevertheless, to keep the quality of the information high also required a rigorous screening process of the contributed documents. We built a structured editing system supporting collaborative publishing (Fig. 2.12).

Different authors are able to simultaneously edit the same document. Once the document is completed, it has to pass quality control. Before it is put on the

Infrastructure	Web Server Operations
	Directory Service
	Security
Authoring Support	Collaborative Publishing
	Layout & Design Guidelines
Navigation	Navigational Framework
	Home Page (Portal)

Figure 2.11   Intranet sub-projects.

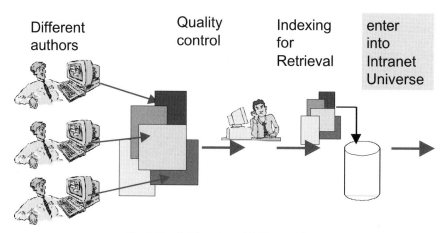

Fig. 2.12   Collaborative publishing workflow.

publicly accessible Web server, the document is indexed for searching. Also, to ensure consistently visually appealing documents, layout and design guidelines are defined that are mandatory for authors. Quality control people check documents for adherence to these guidelines. The content responsibility is placed with the owner for the whole lifetime of a document.

The navigation framework sub-project puts a whole set of browsing and searching tools at the reader's disposal. We applied the four design concepts for navigation described in Section 5.2.3.

(1) We put great effort into defining a meaningful and easy-to-use link structure.
(2) We implemented an Intranet-wide search engine, making sure that the index is always up-to-date.
(3) After some experimentation with automatically created knowledge maps, we manually created different overview maps of the Intranet document universe.
(4) We integrated an advanced commercially available search engine that provides agents for automatic searching.

A lot of effort was also put into the home page of the Intranet, as this is the business card of the company towards the employee. We created a corporate portal that allows users to customize their own home page depending on their own information needs. Search agents automatically collect relevant information that is displayed when users load their personal home page.

We needed to convince our customer that maintaining a corporate Intranet-based portal for knowledge management is a continuous investment.

The chart in Fig. 2.13 illustrates the costs of setting up and maintaining the Intranet. Buying appropriate hardware and software (the bottom light-grey boxes in Fig. 2.13) was the smallest initial investment. Developing a customized knowledge management infrastructure that motivates information sharing required a larger investment (dark boxes in Fig. 2.13). But by far the largest investment is to reward people for putting high-value information on the Intranet. This means, for example, to give employees an internal charge code on which they can book their time when they put information on the Intranet.

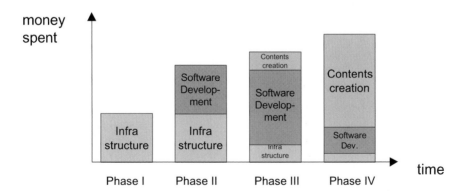

Fig. 2.13 Costs of Intranet setup and maintenance.

The company needs to maintain a permanent staff of not only Web masters, but also of content editors and quality control people.

After an initial setup phase of 6 months, the system is now continuously extended and in daily use by some 1000 users at six different locations in the USA, Japan, and Europe.

2.4.2 Global collaboration by groupware

An international services company wanted to be able to better support their field staff who are working at their clients' premises. The field engineers typically spend a few days at each client site. At the core of our solution is a world-wide replicated Notes database that stores the reports of the field engineers in a standardized format. Data can be fed into the system by a Notes-based front-end running on a PC (Fig. 2.14).

The system can then be used to print out the standardized reports, or to electronically transport extracts of the reports to the IT system of the customers. The following table describes how the system is normally used.

Notes security protection mechanisms were sufficient for our purpose. Additional protection was gained by defining security guidelines for using the system.

In order to streamline business processes and to improve productivity, time, activity, and cost reporting was integrated in our solution. A detailed business process analysis of how to seamlessly integrate the interfacing processes into the work process was conducted in the first project analysis phase. The goal was to make it as simple as possible for the user to enter information into the system.

Our system had to interface to numerous other IT systems. In the analysis phase adequate mechanisms for integrating and exporting data to mainframes

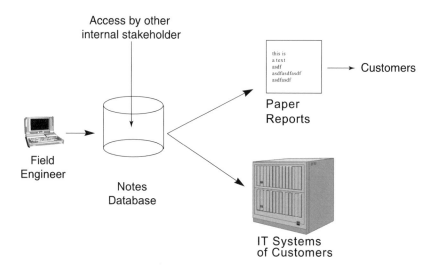

Fig. 2.14 Global collaboration by groupware.

No	Process step	Location	Supporting activity by our system
1	Setup	Office	In the initial step the field engineer gets the assignment with initial information via Lotus Notes in her/his mailbox.
2	Research	Office	The field engineer can collect previous reports from the Notes database and other supporting systems. S/he can also automatically prepare a short questionnaire for the site to be visited that can be e-mailed or faxed to the site manager to be filled out before the field engineer arrives. If there are site plans from previous visits, those can be printed out.
3	Perform work	on-Site	The field engineer works on-site. Background info can be consulted during her/his visit. Geographical marks can be made on the paper site plan.
4	Present	on-Site	The presentation of the results to the site management can be done either verbally or supported by a laptop using the system.
5	Write-Up	Office	In the office the field engineer completes her/his report either by copying paper forms to the system, or by copying information into the system, or by completing information that has been entered into the system using a laptop on-site.
6	Illustrate	Office	Drawings are entered into the system by using a very simple digital drawing and sketching system.
7	Communicate	Office	The results of the on-site work are sent to peer reviewers and all others who need them, using the controlled workflow features of Lotus Notes.
8	Follow-up	Office	Administrative steps, such as time reporting can be completed using our system. Additional follow-up actions can again be triggered using Lotus Notes workflows.

2

were determined. Lotus Notes capabilities were insufficient for the integration of non-textual information into the reports. Office tools were wired in for drawing graphs and calculating statistics.

After more than 1 year of development the system is now successfully used by approximately 500 users working from offices in 22 countries.

2.4.3 Reengineering the core business processes

A medium-sized company asked us to reengineer and implement their core business processes. The company had just gone through a major 2-year reengineering exercise which had been stopped when the new IT system could not made to work reliably. Once started, we therefore assumed that at least the reengineered processes could be relied on and we initially had intended to use a workflow management system to automate the reengineered processes. As it turned out, the processes had to be reengineered again because IT capabilities had progressed so much in the meantime, mainly thanks to the Internet revolution. We also decided against using a general-purpose workflow management system and chose to use a package (Siebel).

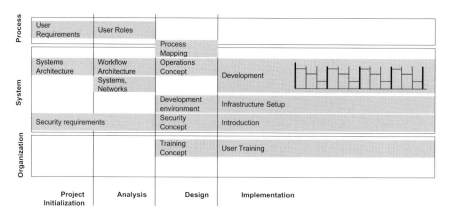

Fig. 2.15 Business process implementation.

Figure 2.15 describes graphically how we organized the project. Unfortunately, this project did not get over the analysis phase. After 1 year of project work, our customer was bought by a much larger competitor. We only built a feasibility prototype, because as a result of the sale of the company, all reengineering efforts were put on hold.

2.4.4. Supply chain optimization in the pharmaceutical industry

Most pharmaceutical companies are currently involved in supply chain optimization projects. Because many of the leading companies have been involved in mergers over the last few years, their supply chains need to be reengineered in any case. The efficiency and harmonization are not good enough in a number of areas and so this opens up a huge potential for savings.

In the pharmaceutical industry, as in other domains, there are no longer sequential supply chains, but rather supply networks. The supply network is composed of a network of suppliers of raw material, a network of production units existing within the company or as external units, a network of distributors, wholesalers, pharmacies and even a network of doctors and a network of patients (Fig. 2.16).

Pharmaceutical companies will need to deal with different groups such as hospitals, e-pharmacies, doctors and patients. The main communication means is increasingly the Internet. Orders from e-pharmacies will be placed on the Internet, the delivery date will be confirmed and the order will be processed by the distribution system of the manufacturing company. Also, transport organizations will need to be tightly integrated. Pharmaceutical companies will need to provide a seamless information flow between production, distribution, e-Pharmacies and the consumer. This means that the whole supply network will need to be integrated using technologies such as Internet-based supply chain optimization systems from vendors like I2 or manugistics.

Two of the main e-business developments that pharmaceutical companies will have to deal with are on-line pharmacies and dedicated chemical Internet market places.

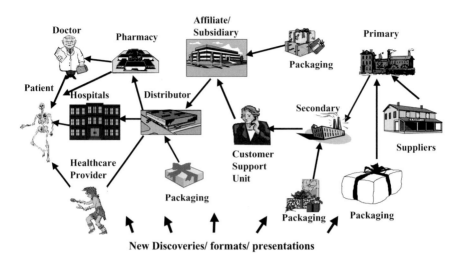

Fig. 2.16   Pharmaceutical supply network (source: i2 Technologies).

New sales channels

On-line pharmacies have been mushrooming in the recent past. Customers have rapidly switched from "real" pharmacies, because ordering from an on-line pharmacy is much more convenient. In the USA, the large pharmacy chains such as Walgreens (www.walgreens.com) and CVS (www.cvs.com) offer on-line refills and sell some articles directly over the Web. In an effort to attract or at least retain customers, CVS even offers free shipping. Nevertheless, dedicated on-line pharmacy portals such as drugstore.com or PlanetRX (www.planetrx.com) have much more comprehensive services. PlanetRX, for example, besides offering a huge global on-line inventory, provides many value added services. It offers product advice, such as how to treat acne and has a big database of drug information. It also gives its users the opportunity to ask a real pharmacist questions by e-mail. PlanetRX promises to answer these questions within 24 hours. It hosts virtual communities of shared interested, for example about arthritis or depression. PlanetRx tries to create an on-line community feeling by offering on-line chat, a message board, and by hosting special guests.

Chemical Internet market places

Chemdex (www.chemdex.com) calls itself the leading life science e-commerce marketplace. It is representative of a new brand of industry-specific on-line marketplaces on the Internet. Chemdex caters to three different user groups.

- Purchasing professionals, who buy chemical ingredients for their company, get simplified procurement processes.
- Scientists and researchers, who are looking for a particular chemical substance, get a one-stop-shop containing hundreds of thousands of life science products.

- Chemical suppliers get cheap access to a global sales and distribution channel.

Chemdex also offers full outsourcing of procurement including the company-specific approval workflow on behalf of client companies.

Technology aspects

The pharmaceutical industry is embracing XML as the enabler for EDI over the Internet. Various XML dictionaries for chemical applications (for example cXML) are under development by vendors and standardization organizations. The pharmaceutical industry also has high security requirements, because communication between doctors and patients is highly confidential. To send prescriptions over the Web, and to order refills from on-line pharmacies, digital certificates are used for patient authentication. In the area of e-Procurement, most pharmaceutical companies have reengineering initiatives under way, where the optimized procurement processes will be automated by tools from vendors such as Ariba or CommerceOne.

The pharmaceutical industry is moving towards seamless integration of its business processes, extending from buying and selling (galenical) ingredients at chemical Internet marketplaces to directly handling the delivery to patients on behalf of on-line pharmacies. At the same time, non-core activities are outsourced to external service providers, to focus on core competencies such as research, product development, and marketing.

2.5 Case study: dating over the Web

It has always been easy to make money using human wishes, hopes, and desires! The dating industry, which is heavily fragmented and exhibits many small entrepreneurs, has been one of the earliest adopters of information technology. Computer-based matchmaking was one of the earliest PC applications. People had to fill out questionnaires with their profiles, which were entered into databases. Profiles of candidates in search of spouses were matched against profiles in the database. Matchmaking is a classical example for the application of Metcalfe's law, which says that the usefulness of any network grows exponentially with the number of people participating in it. The Internet with its potential of hundreds of millions of users is the ideal environment for this sort of application.

Web dating companies have been among the earliest adopters of Web technology. They very successfully operate as middlemen, making money of their database of love-seeking people. Web dating companies operate as knowledge facilitators and mediators, successfully turning data (a user's personal records) into information (a virtual personality) into knowledge (putting two virtual personalities in touch with each other). The larger their databases, the better the chances that they can offer a matching person to the love seeker. They therefore try to entice casual browsers to enter their personal information into their databases. The largest services claim to have millions of users in their databases. They then try to turn this information into profit by charging users for accessing the databases. Users specify what they are searching for, and get back a listing of people that they might find interesting. Sometimes, Web dating companies already charge for making searches, but the clever ones return the listing of potential candidates, only blocking out the contact information. The customer then needs to pay to send e-mail to the candidate.

2.5.1 Using leading-edge technology

To make their systems as easy to use as possible, Web dating companies are early adopters of advanced user interface and search technologies. They collect information in structured and semi-structured format. Figure 2.17 displays the data collection form of DatingClub.com. This form makes it very easy to enter information. The information collected is also robust to errors and simple to search.

For instantaneous matchmaking, dating companies successfully employ on-line chat and virtual reality technologies. This means, that members can get in touch with each other on-line. Figure 2.18 displays a very simple to use on-line chat room of adultfriendfinder.com. People interested in getting instantaneous contact can enter the chat room and get in touch with others in public. They then have the chance to enter a closed chat room for a private conversation.

The webpersonals.com Web site combines on-line listings and real-time communication by chatting in a intuitive way, putting short profiles of on-line people and a chat window on the same screen (Fig. 2.19). To talk to somebody who is on-line, people need to buy credits from webpersonals.com.

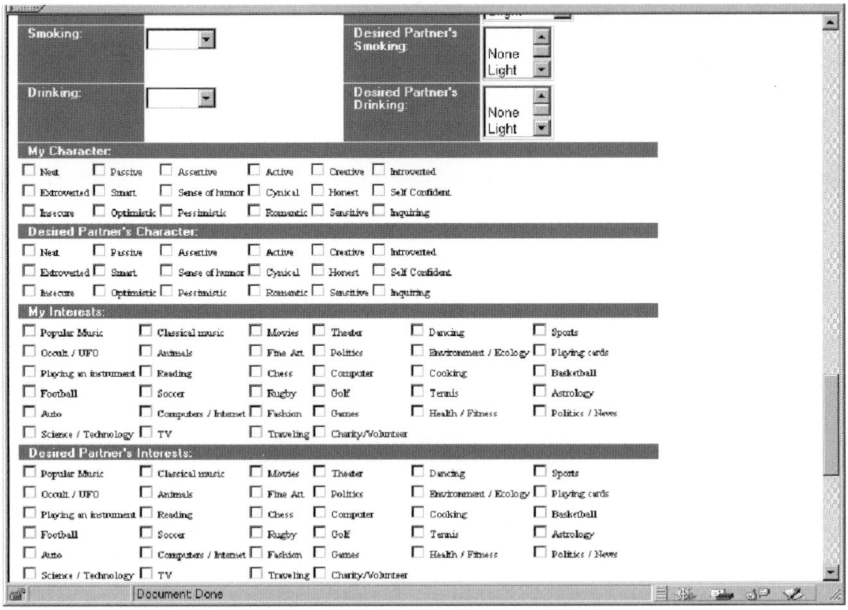

Fig. 2.17 DatingClub.com user input screen.

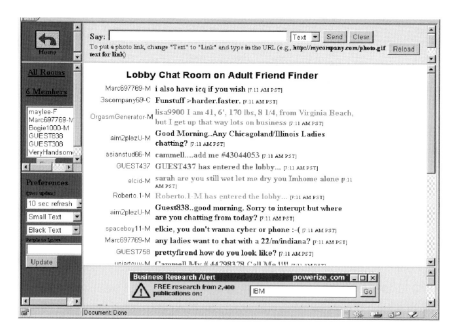

Fig. 2.18 "Lobby" chat room of adultfriendfinder.com.

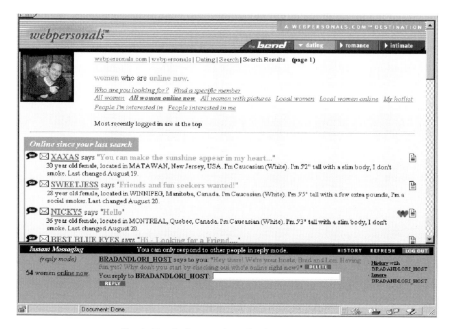

Fig. 2.19 On-line window of webpersonals.com.

To find people, Web dating companies are also employing sophisticated search techniques. Besides easy-to-use browsing and searching forms, dating companies use powerful searching techniques, where new matches are offered based on ratings of previous matches that readers have looked at. For example, adultfriendfinder has a matching system that can automatically figure out what type of people somebody likes among the thousands of members. Users can comment on a few members by going to some profiles they like and rate them by clicking on one of the comment buttons in the middle of the page (Fig. 2.20).

Users get then back a ranked listing of profiles of candidates that might be of interest to them.

Other services use agent technology to scan the entire database of candidates periodically on changes and additions that might be of interest to the subscriber. The Agent-of-love scans its database daily and mails every night a listing of people that might be of interest to the subscriber. The subscriber can then directly get in touch with the person that has advertised her/himself, first by anonymous e-mail, later directly when mutual trust has been established.

2.5.2 Using innovative business models

The Web dating industry has been very creative in optimizing income by successfully selling the most volatile of goods, information. This is even more amazing because people are paying for the good to which they are actually contributing, namely their own personal information. Web dating companies are archetypal information brokers or infomediaries, which do not create information themselves. Rather, their added value consists of linking buyers of

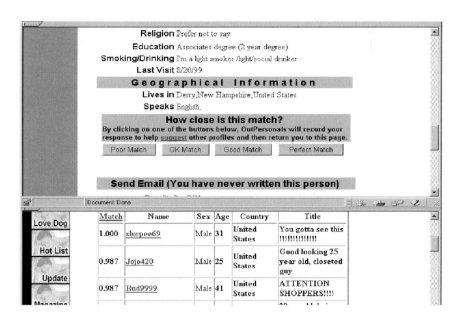

Fig. 2.20 Rating on profiles on adultfriendfinder.com.

information with vendors of information. They employ the same business model as on-line auction house eBay that is linking buyers and sellers of physical goods. The particularity of a Web dating community is that each buyer is also a vendor, and that vendors are "putting up themselves for sale"!

There are two different models of dating services. The "information push" type dating services distribute periodical lists of new candidates that have the same interests as the person looking for a match. The "information pull" type dating services provide a virtual meeting place where people can interactively browse profiles, or engage in real-time interaction in a chat forum. Some Web sites provide combinations of the two types.

The basic principle of both types of dating services is the same: The customer pays rent to the dating service for setting up and administrating a virtual meeting place in cyberspace. Customers will flock to the dating service that is providing the best virtual meeting place, where the best people are to be found. The challenge for the dating service is to get the customer to stick to their site, i.e. to become a portal. The best way to get customer loyalty is to have a huge, rapidly growing, and active virtual community that preferably goes on-line daily. The growing user base will provide new daily matches for the regular user, which in turn makes it more engaging for the user to stay on-line. A huge user base to start with makes it more attractive for new users to join, because they will get a large collection of potential matches to start with.

This means that a dating service has to "grow or perish" (Fig. 2.21). This also means that the on-going concentration process will accelerate in the future. These are typical symptoms for Web-based industries.

Dating services utilize different strategies to optimize income (Table 2.1). Adding one's personality profile to the database is usually free, because dating services have a vital interested in growing the user base as quickly as possible. People that have entered their information can then wait for free until somebody else gets in touch with them. Being the active part in getting in touch, on the other hand, is usually quite costly. The art for the dating service is to make the free part attractive enough to entice people to enter their profile and then offer enough incentive to have their users pay for becoming more active and, for example, do searches for pay. Dating services employ two fundamentally different strategies:

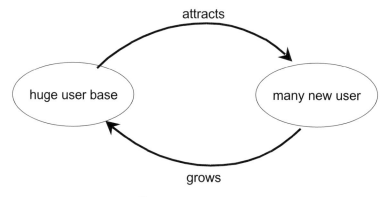

Fig. 2.21 Grow or perish.

Table 2.1 Revenue models of sample dating services

Dating Service	Become a member (enter info)	Teaser (free services)	Revenue model
DatingClub	Free	Browse first 100 listings, searching is free	Pay per period for accessing full profiles
Webpersonals	Free	Browsing/searching is free	Pay each time for contacting other members
Match	Free	All services for initial period	Pay per period for all services
Adultfriendfinder	Free	First three viewings of profiles per day free	Pay per period for browsing/ searching/contacting other members
Agent-of-love	Free	Profiles mailed to user daily	Pay per period for contacting other members

2

- Charge a flat fee for using the services for a fixed period of time. This strategy can be refined by offering a basic set of services for a lower fee, while selling "gold" memberships with additional privileges for a higher price.
- Charge for each message sent to another user. This is similar to long-distance phone companies that charge for connect time. Dating services charge for sending e-mail messages, but also for connect time in chat sessions.

Dating services exhibit the e-business-typical combination of global accessibility and local relationships. Candidates can access any profile on the globe, but they are much more likely to contact people in their physical neighbourhood. Dating services therefore either try to get global coverage, or they try to get an extensive user base in selected geographical areas.

2.6 Critical success factors for e-business transformation

Dating services exhibit all of the vital criteria of a typical e-business:

- The user interface and searching functionality is essential for success!
- Create virtual communities!
- Grow or perish!
- Give away information to create new business!
- Think global, act local!
- Innovate! Innovate! Innovate!

To successfully transform a business into an e-business, there are a few fundamental principles to follow. First of all, in order to transform a business, a company needs to *understand what its current business is*. To convert the business, best practice e-business processes can then be compared to the "as is" processes. The most critical information for a company is knowledge about its core business. This knowledge is in the form of process knowledge about its business processes and domain knowledge about the general business domain. Everything else besides managing this core knowledge can be outsourced. e-Business technologies greatly support outsourcing of business processes, leaving the augmentation of core knowledge as the main challenge for the company. To succeed in the e-business economy, information needs to flow freely and bi-directionally between all parts of the company. Information must be made accessible to everyone who needs it. To attract customers and create new business, companies need to make a careful decision about *what critical information of added value to the customer they might want to give away.*

e-Business leaders like Dell or Amazon display a clear tendency towards a reduction of their business to the core competencies. The most successful big enterprises split their business into autonomous cells, delegating competencies to people at the front who deal with the daily business. To succeed in complex tasks, e-business supports the setting up of virtual structures that are assembled for a particular task, and are disbanded afterwards. Service providers that offer non-critical business functions as their core competency will be among the crucial building blocks for these "ad hoc" companies.

The e-business economy also displays a *discrepancy between the global nature of the Internet* and the fact that it is time-consuming and *expensive to move people and goods over long distances.* Companies that exploit this discrepancy will be among the e-business leaders.

3 *Blueprint for e-business implementation*

Introduction	Definitions of: ▶ e-Commerce ▶ e-Business ▶ Knowledge management
1 Dispelling the myths of e-business	▶ Income gaps between industrialized countries and 3rd World ▶ Re-distribution of wealth in society ▶ Isolation of individual
2 Turning business into e-business	▶ e-Business transformation ▶ Business process outsourcing ▶ Portals ▶ Case study: pharmaceutical industry ▶ Case study: dating over the Web
3 Blueprint for e-business implementation	▶ **The information process integration blueprint** ▶ **e-Business deployment roadmap** ▶ **Knowledge management deployment** ▶ **e-Business project management**
4 Key e-business technologies	▶ XML overview ▶ Security and digital money ▶ Virtual collaboration ▶ Workflow management ▶ Process integration by packageware
5 Tools for managing knowledge	▶ MIT process handbook ▶ Knowledge navigation

3

> The Information Process Integration (IPI) Blueprint describes the main steps of converting a business to e-business. The e-business deployment roadmap lists the main milestones that need to be taken care of and identifies the most common roadblocks on the journey towards e-business. Introducing a knowledge management strategy and its associated tools is an integral part of the e-business transformation. The chapter concludes by reviewing common observations about how to manage an e-business project.
> This chapter discusses the following topics:
> ● The InformationProcessIntegration Blueprint
> ● e-Business deployment roadmap
> ● Knowledge management deployment
> ● e-Business project management.

The previous chapter has shown that e-business transformation can be successfully implemented in two ways. It can either succeed top-down, by changing the business strategy and processes to make full use of the Internet and its associated technologies, or it can be done bottom-up, by employing new IT tools to dramatically speed up existing processes. On their journey to becoming a full-fledged e-business company whose business model makes full use of all facets of Internet technology, we can distinguish companies in four stages (Fig. 3.1).

● At stage one, the goal for a company is just to put up an external Web site where it usually publishes marketing material.

● At stage two, the company tries to involve the Web customer in a dialogue by providing interactive information such as the opportunity to order brochures on-line.

● At stage three, a company is engaging its customers in e-commerce, selling goods and services over the Web, or offering on-line customer services.

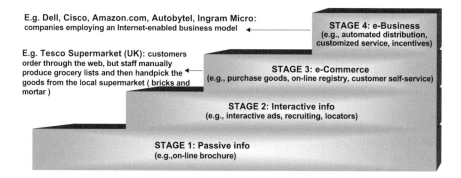

Fig. 3.1 The four stages of e-transformation (source: Deloitte Consulting).

- At stage four, a business becomes a true e-business, employing one of the business models described in Section 2.1.3. Companies like Dell, Amazon, or CISCO fall in this category.

3.1 The IPI blueprint

If a company has decided to embark on the journey towards e-business, common-sense recommends starting simply, and progressively delving into the deeper mysteries and complexities of e-business. Based on numerous e-business transformation projects in different industries and for companies of varying size, we have come up with a simple blueprint for e-business transformation. We call this blueprint "Information Process Integration" blueprint, or short, IPI blueprint (Fig. 3.2).

The IPI blueprint starts on the first level by *making information accessible* to anyone who needs it. The simplest, cheapest, and quickest means for making information accessible is a company-wide Intranet. To collect experience, we recommend putting non-business critical information such as the internal phone book, or some manuals, on the Intranet first. As soon as the Intranet is operational, business-critical information such as marketing and sales information or product management information should also be put on the Intranet. To harness the full information management capabilities of the Intranet, technologies such as document management, information retrieval, but also knowledge management tools need to be deployed.

At the same time, an external Web site for information dissemination should be set up. It is important not just to put up the company brochure to say "we are here!", but to add real value. If we want repeat customers on the Web site, new contents should be added periodically.

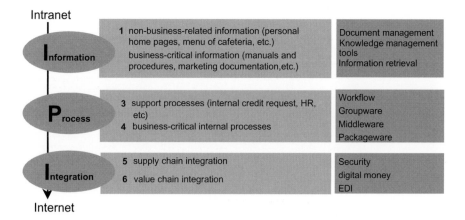

Fig. 3.2 The Information Process Integration blueprint.

The second level of the IPI blueprint deals with *process automation*. Internet-related and Internet-enabled technologies such as workflow and groupware are the basic building blocks to integrate and optimize company-wide business processes. If the business model permits, software packages should be used, such as SAP for enterprise resource planning or Siebel for sales and marketing. To integrate heterogeneous applications ranging from host-based legacy applications, over client/server applications to object-oriented software, middleware systems such as transaction monitors, message queuing servers, or object request brokers can be used.

At the same time, we might want to consider using the Web as a sales channel to start selling our products over the Internet. We also might want to give our clients an opportunity to get in touch with us over the Web.

The third level of the IPI blueprint covers *integration of business processes* over company boundaries. The Internet enables integration at an unprecedented level, either by using packages such as I2, Ariba, SAP, or Siebel, or by utilizing open standards such as XML and other Internet protocols (see Chapter 4). One obvious area for integration is the supply chain, but the whole value chain should be optimized using the Internet as an integration medium. At this level, technologies such as EDI over the Internet, security applications such as authentication by digital certificates, and digital payment systems need to be utilized.

On each of the three IPI levels, an identical framework for analysis and design can be used. Once the overall e-business strategy has been defined, the four core business areas, namely buying and selling, design and production, learning and change, and management and decision making (Fig. 3.3) can be addressed separately.

Once a company has transformed itself into an e-business, it can be described using the three-layer e-business architecture (Fig. 3.4).

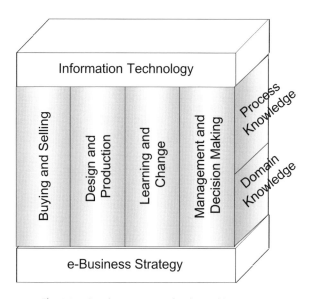

Fig. 3.3 Core business areas for the IPI blueprint.

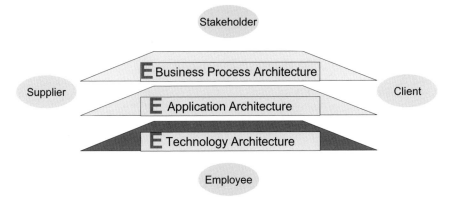

Fig. 3.4   e-Business three-layer architecture.

On the first layer, the process layer, the e-business process architecture is mapped. As shown in Fig. 3.5, the new product creation process is at the centre of the company's business. On the buy side, processes to the suppliers should be integrated seamlessly. On the sell side, customer care processes should be similarly augmented by using Internet technologies. Stakeholder information can be readily made accessible on the company's Web site. Besides using the company's core ERP systems for their daily work, employees can now get direct access to the company's administrative information.

Figure 3.6 contains a detailed listing of all processes that can be supported by e-business at the buy side, inside, and at the sell side.

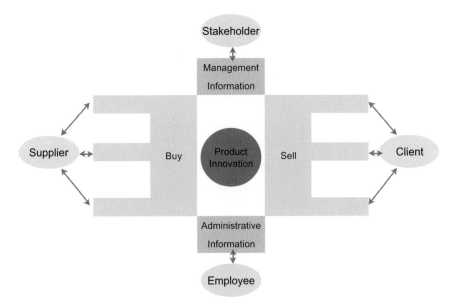

Fig. 3.5   e-Business process architecture.

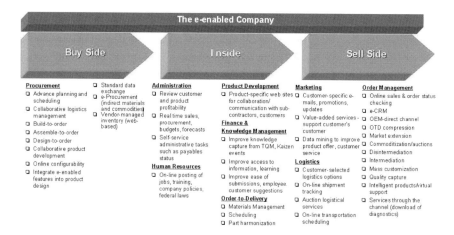

Fig. 3.6   e-Enabled processes inside and at the outside of a company (source: Deloitte Consulting).

The business processes of the top layer are automated using the software packages on the middle layer, the business application architecture (Fig. 3.7). On the buy side, processes between the suppliers and the company can be integrated using Internet technologies. Procurement is automated by packages from vendors such as Ariba or CommerceOne, production processes can be integrated along the supply chain using mainstream ERP packages such as SAP, PeopleSoft, Oracle, or Baan, and distribution and logistics processes can be integrated using the services of global distributors such as UPS or Fedex.

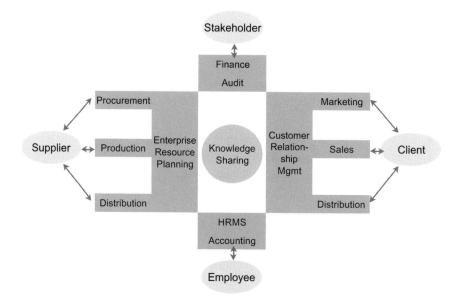

Fig. 3.7   e-Business application architecture.

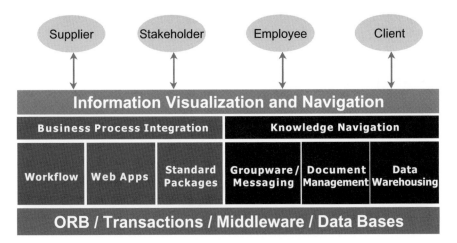

Fig. 3.8   e-Business systems architecture.

In the centre of the company are the processes to manage change and learning. This is the area where there are the least software packages available. While there are Internet-based tools for knowledge management available (see Chapter 5), it is most important to nurture a company culture that values the sharing of knowledge. On the sell side, customer relationship management systems like Siebel can support the sales force in its sales and marketing efforts. Tools like Broadvision help in setting up a sophisticated Web sales presence.

On the lowest layer of the e-business three-layer architecture is the systems architecture (Fig. 3.8). The systems architecture describes the IT tools and technologies that make up the physical IT landscape. The components of this architecture are discussed in Chapter 4.

3.2   e-Business deployment roadmap

Once a company has decided to embark on the e-business journey, a roadmap for deployment needs to be prepared. It is of fundamental importance to consider business and IT aspects from the very beginning.

When the overall business vision is defined, business and IT experts should work together to get a complete vision covering all aspects of the business and fully harnessing the potential of e-business technology (Fig. 3.9). In the beginning, business experts do the lion's share of the work, while IT experts give input to extend and complete the vision. During the course of the e-business journey, the role of the IT experts steadily expands, while business experts play a crucial role in quality control to make sure that the IT system fulfils the business requirements. The circle in the background of Fig. 3.9 indicates the iterative nature of the e-transformation process, which is never completed, but rather an on-going activity. During the e-transformation

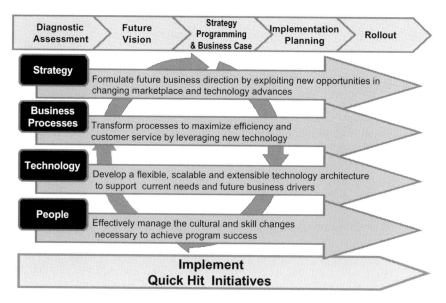

Fig. 3.9 Sample roadmap for e-transformation (source: Deloitte Consulting).

process, numerous opportunities for "quick hit" initiatives will come up. These can be process automation projects, or opportunities for Internet spin-offs.

An e-business vision detailed into an e-business strategy consists of three orthogonal components (Fig. 3.10).

- The first component, the business strategy, is based on the core competency of the company, such as selling books, assembling computers, or producing drugs.
- The second component, the knowledge management strategy, describes how the domain-specific knowledge and knowledge about the core business processes should be managed.
- The third component, the IT strategy, describes the IT systems and tools that should be used to implement the business and knowledge management strategies.

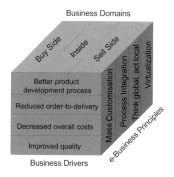

Fig. 3.10 The three parts of an e-business strategy.

Putting together the pieces listed in the IPI blueprint results in the e-business deployment roadmap depicted in Fig. 3.11. It outlines the process of how the e-business vision can be implemented. Any vision for even the most mundane businesses should consider the e-business aspects and therefore this is called e-business vision in Fig. 3.11.

The implementation of the business strategy is composed of the three parts

- business strategy,
- knowledge management strategy, and
- IT strategy.

On the business process level, the four core business areas from the IPI blueprint should be fleshed out.

- For the design and production area, supply chain management and procurement processes need to be specified and automated with packages from vendors like SAP, I2, or Ariba.
- In the sales and marketing area, electronic customer care processes have to be specified and automated with tools like Siebel or Vantive.
- For the learning and change area, there are many tacitly known processes that can only be manually automated with groupware, messaging, and document management tools.
- Data warehousing and MIS tools support the management and decision making processes. The specification of a general messaging infrastructure,

3

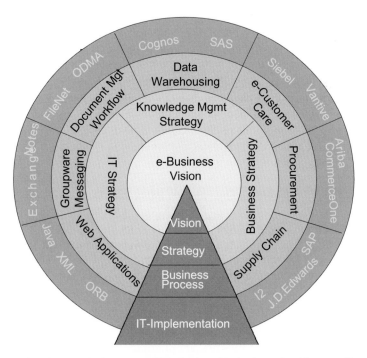

Fig. 3.11   The e-business deployment roadmap (tools and technologies listed here are discussed in Chapters 4 and 5).

	Business Process	Knowledge Mgmt	IT
Vision		e-Business Vision	
Strategy	Business Strategy	KM Strategy	IT Strategy
Process	BPR Process Mapping	K Navigation K Map	Analysis & Design
Delivery	Supply Chain Customer Care Procurement	Messaging Groupware Data Warehousing	Workflow Document Management Web Apps

Fig. 3.12   e-Business deployment roadmap as a table.

of a Web application development environment, and of middleware such as workflow management systems is part of the IT strategy.

Figure 3.12 displays the same roadmap in table format, listing the major activities for each phase in the e-business deployment process. In the process definition phase, the business process specification component has as its end product a process map that can, for example, be described and stored in the Process Handbook discussed in Chapter 5. In the process definition phase, the knowledge management component has as the final product a knowledge map of the explicit knowledge needed to realize the e-business vision.

While there are many books and methods available for process mapping, there are no such tools and methods for knowledge mapping. The next section therefore briefly discusses this fundamentally important subject.

3.3   Knowledge management deployment

Knowledge management deployment starts at the strategy level. Whether a company decides to create a Chief Knowledge Officer position at all does not matter so much as whether the company recognizes that knowledge is a critical asset of strategic importance which needs to be appropriately managed. A knowledge management strategy looks at issues like intellectual asset valuation and management (Fig. 3.13). An example of this is consciously managing things like a company's patents.

The most fundamental issue is to nurture an organization and a culture that value sharing of knowledge. Knowledge sharing can be facilitated, for example, by setting up virtual communities about topics that are of interest to the company. Moderators of these virtual communities need to be appropriately rewarded for contributing time, energy, and knowledge to the operation of the

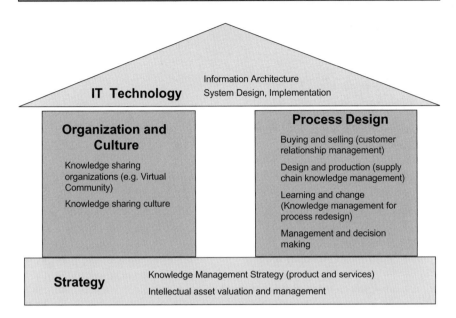

Fig. 3.13 Knowledge management deployment issues.

3

virtual community. The four core business areas (see Fig. 3.3) need also to be supported by appropriate knowledge management concepts and systems, setting up knowledge management systems for sales and marketing, design and production, learning and change, and management and decision making. To support managing knowledge by information technology, an appropriate information infrastructure based on an Intranet needs to be put into place.

3.3.1 Knowledge mapping

Creating comprehensive knowledge maps for a certain topic can be as simple as having a Rolodex with the addresses of the people knowledgeable in the topic. In practice, however, IT systems are used to produce graphical overview maps of the databases and documents about a certain topic. Tools and techniques for knowledge mapping are described in Chapter 5.

For each topic, we should again distinguish between domain knowledge and process knowledge. Domain knowledge is about understanding the nature, location and owners of existing knowledge resources (e.g. people, databases, libraries, etc.) across the organization. The result of the knowledge mapping activity is a map of the domain knowledge resources, which can be used as a guide for knowledge access. During the knowledge mapping process, an analysis of the needs and gaps leads to an action plan for addressing these gaps in a firm-wide knowledge management system.

Mapping process knowledge leads to an understanding of the flow of knowledge across the business processes. The result is a process map of the work-based knowledge flow. During the knowledge mapping process, an assessment of what knowledge is generated and where it is needed should be performed. An analysis of the needs and gaps should lead to an action plan for closing these gaps.

3.4 e-Business project management: new concepts, old obstacles!

Managing an e-business project is not so different from managing other IT projects. The basic project management model still is derived from the waterfall model (Fig. 3.14). For each e-business project, first an analysis of the requirements needs to be made, then the solution has to be designed and implemented. As with all software projects, it is of fundamental importance to thoroughly test the completed solution before it is deployed on a large scale.

e-Business projects follow a variant of the waterfall model that first gained widespread popularity for the realization of object-oriented systems. The spiral model for project management describes a prototyping-oriented approach, where a succession of prototypes is developed rapidly, to be verified and refined under heavy user testing (Fig. 3.15). User feedback is then incorporated into the next prototype, until it is decided to turn the last prototype into the production system.

Developing projects the e-business way thus follows the object-oriented life cycle:

- Analyze a little.
- Design a little.
- Implement a little.
- Test a little.
- Start over again.

As time to market is absolutely crucial in the fast-paced Internet age, this evolutionary implementation approach allows a company to rapidly put the parts of its new system into use as they become available for deployment. This

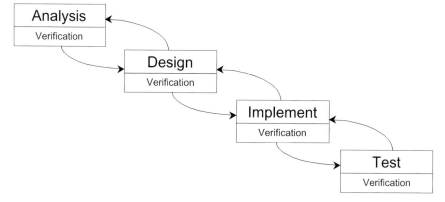

Fig. 3.14 The waterfall model is still valid.

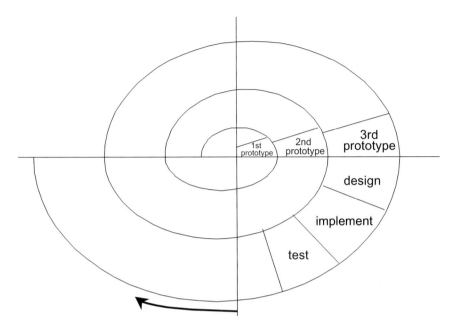

Fig. 3.15   The spiral model comes into play.

3

allows continuously refining each part, even abolishing it and re-inventing a new solution if the market demands it.

It cannot be forgotten that e-business deployment is software deployment. In the area of software engineering, the silver bullet has been announced many times before. First, structured programming was been touted as the solution to the software engineering crisis. Later, after it became apparent that structured programming would not solve all the problems, object-oriented programming was the solution, converting "everything" into an object. Currently, agent-based programming is considered the "silver bullet" of software development, which means that the agent metaphor is indiscriminately applied to all software development activities. Other software development fads are also offered as ideal tools, techniques or methods to build e-business systems. Artificial intelligence techniques have been around for decades, unfortunately they have had only limited success in narrowly defined problem areas. Technologies like fuzzy logic promise to better model the fuzziness of reality, while neural networks are supposed to model the inner workings of the human brain. But even with all of these innovative approaches, the old problems still do persist. Building successful IT systems is still much more of an art than of a science! All the new software engineering, development, and management tools and methods such as object-oriented programming, design patterns, CASE (computer-aided software engineering), or software metrics, have not greatly increased overall productivity.

The biggest improvement in productivity and overall software quality can be achieved by improving the quality of the production process. Although there has been substantial effort in defining software quality by organizations like

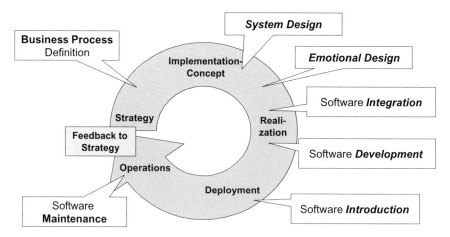

Fig. 3.16 The continuous process project model.

ISO (the International Standards Organization), this does not mean that the quality of software has greatly improved over the past 10–20 years. The most marked improvement (Glass, 1999) has not come by introducing any new tools, but by applying the so-called capability maturity model from the Carnegie–Mellon Software Engineering Institute with its five process levels. This means that soft factors, such as improving the process of software production, provide by far the greatest improvement in software quality.

Having dedicated, knowledgeable, and motivated people is still the most crucial success factor for an e-business project.

Combining the waterfall model and the spiral model leads to the continuous process project model for e-business projects. After defining the strategy, the business process to be automated has to be designed. Afterwards, the implementation concept is written, leading to the design of the IT system. One particularity of e-business systems is the importance of the user interface. The GUI is developed in the emotional design phase, which is highly significant for the usability of the final system. Thereafter, the system is assembled, combining as many prefabricated pieces as possible. Missing software parts need to be developed. Subsequently, the system is deployed and introduced. Once it is operational, it goes into the maintenance phase. And then it is extremely important to keep the feedback loop open, to be ready for new developments, to make adjustments to the strategy or even be prepared to come up with a new strategy and start the whole process all over again from the beginning.

3.4.1 Sample e-business deployment: the Chinese gift shop

This section illustrates the e-business deployment process by describing the activities needed to set up a simple Web-based shop for selling high-quality Chinese gifts.

Vision

The mission of the shop is to provide Chinese gifts of high cultural value at an excellent price to customers anywhere on the globe by setting up an Internet shop for Chinese gifts.

Strategy

The strategy of the gifts shop operators is to team up with Chinese producers of high-quality cultural gifts. They plan to offer a broad selection of best-in-class products at an excellent price, cutting out the importers. They intend to build up a network of Chinese agents scanning the Chinese countryside for new and unique products. They also want to stick to these core competencies and to outsource as much of the non-business-critical activities as possible.

USP (unique selling proposition)

They think that they have a unique direct link to first-class providers of Chinese cultural gifts. They want to implement a seamlessly integrated Web site handling the whole business process on-line. They intend to provide added value by including expert social, historical, and cultural background information with each shipped product.

Risks

One of the main risks associated with setting up this business is that their content providers, that is the Chinese gift producers, could set up the Internet mall themselves. Another major risk is that the content providers might collect the addresses of the customers and use them to directly address their customers, cutting out the Internet mall.

Because the computer literacy and Internet penetration of Chinese craftsmen is low, the Internet gift shop team deems this risk relatively low and decides to go ahead with its plans.

Major business processes

Figure 3.17 contains the high level specification of the major business processes for operating the Internet mall. These processes now need to be implemented applying the e-business Deployment Roadmap in the four main business areas.

3.5 Critical success factors for e-business project management

Successfully managing an e-business transformation project follows the same fundamental rules as for any project. *The waterfall model* is still valid, which means that in spite of all of the exciting new prototyping capabilities of the Internet tools, analysis and design phases are needed for each serious project. However, there are some points that are of particular importance to an e-

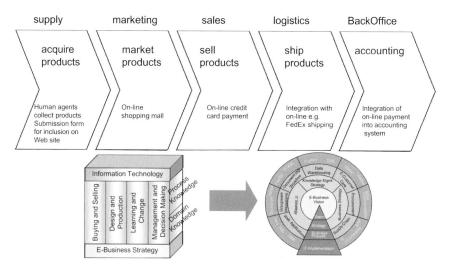

Fig. 3.17   Business processes for setting up an Internet mall for Chinese gifts.

business project. It is important to have a *team composed of business and IT experts* from the start to the end of the project. For the sake of simplicity and cost effectiveness, as many packages as possible should be used. For all business areas – except for learning and change – packages are available. Custom development can only be justified if the problem is so simple that it can be solved more efficiently with a standard tool such as a groupware tool (for example Lotus Notes) or an office productivity tool (for example Microsoft Excel). The other justification for custom development is if a company can get a competitive advantage in a business-critical area by doing things differently from the competition.

Because deploying e-business normally also means deploying software, the most simple rule of software project management should be applied: only install and put into place software modules that have been *thoroughly tested* in isolation and in combination. Under normal circumstances, only software applications that have been seen running before at another place should be utilized. Sometimes, to be a leader, it can be worthwhile to be the first reference customer for a new software application. In this case, the company needs to be extremely cautious of time and cost overruns, constantly updating planning and revising estimates. Usually, it is much safer to check with other reference customers that have installed exactly the same version of the software.

To staff e-business projects, only the best people should be employed, be they subject-matter experts, computer programmers, or project managers. Top-level management support is absolutely crucial for the success of an e-business project. While the CIO can sponsor an evolutionary bottom-up e-business automation project, such as introducing electronic document management, the CEO needs to put her full engagement behind revolutionary top-down e-business transformation. To cannibalize its own business by, for example, setting up a competing sales channel over the Internet needs the *full commitment* and internal sales effort of the entire *senior management*.

e-Business projects are always integration projects, linking the workflow of business processes over the Internet. Integration is fiendishly complex because adding another system always means adding a new interface to each existing component of the old system. For an integration project as a rule of thumb, the most realistic and pessimistic estimates should, in the end, be doubled. Applying this simple rule will let you manage projects on time and on budget.

After this overview of how to manage the e-business transformation process, the next chapter explores the e-business technologies that enable this transformation process.

3

4 *Key e-business technologies*

Introduction	Definitions of: ▶ e-Commerce ▶ e-Business ▶ Knowledge management
1 Dispelling the myths of e-business	▶ Income gaps between industrialized countries and 3rd World ▶ Re-distribution of wealth in society ▶ Isolation of individual
2 Turning business into e-business	▶ e-Business transformation ▶ Business process outsourcing ▶ Portals ▶ Case study: pharmaceutical industry ▶ Case study: dating over the Web
3 Blueprint for e-business implementation	▶ The information process integration blueprint ▶ e-Business deployment roadmap ▶ Knowledge management deployment ▶ e-Business project management
4 Key e-business technologies	▶ **XML overview** ▶ **Security and digital money** ▶ **Virtual collaboration** ▶ **Workflow management** ▶ **Process integration by packageware**
5 Tools for managing knowledge	▶ MIT process handbook ▶ Knowledge navigation

4

e-Business is a revolution driven by technology. Managers need to know what the IT technology enablers for their business area are. This chapter provides a comprehensive introduction for non-IT professionals. Business processes are now integrated between companies by gluing together the process workflow over the Internet. The automation and integration of these business processes increasingly happens by packageware.

This chapter discusses the following topics:
- e-Business technology overview
- XML overview
- Virtual collaboration
- Workflow management
- Process integration by packageware

The Internet and its associated technologies have turned established enterprises upside-down and created new businesses that would have never been thought of just a few years ago. Just look at the financial industry where on-line stockbrokers like Charles Schwab and E*TRADE have overtaken well-established financial heavyweights like Merril Lynch. Any company that wants to survive in today's hypercompetitive e-business landscape needs to investigate the implications of these new technologies for their business environment. Managers need to assess for themselves the impact of these new technologies for their own business. This chapter gives a survey of the latest developments in associated e-business technologies, enabling business leaders to evaluate the use of these technologies for their own companies.

4.1 e-Business technology overview

Because processes integrated by e-business include all sorts of IT systems and applications, it is well worth looking at the general architecture of current client/server systems, independently of whether these systems include packageware such as SAP, Siebel, or Ariba, or whether they have been custom-built to solve a specific business problem. A state-of-the art IT system usually is built based on the three-tier architecture.

4.1.1 Three-tier architecture

In the past 10 years IT systems have moved from monolithic mainframe-based systems to client/server systems, where the GUI (graphical user interface) resides on the client, while the business logic and main data storage resides on the server.

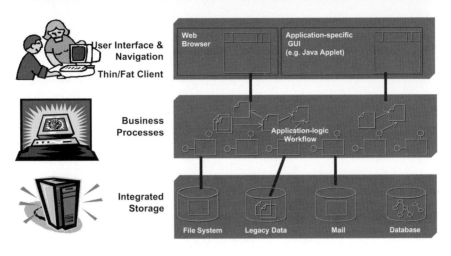

Fig. 4.1 Three-tier client/server architecture.

For state-of-the art Internet-enabled applications, a three-tier client/server architecture is normally used (Fig. 4.1).

- The GUI is implemented in the first tier, either on a thin or a fat client. A "thin" client, such as a network computer, displays the application front end in a Web Browser, or in an application specific GUI. A "fat" client, normally a PC, offers local data processing capabilities, besides providing the same functionality as a thin client.
- The process logic of the business processes is running on the middle tier on the local server. Sometimes, middle-tier business logic is integrated on fat clients. This is where, for example, routing of messages happens, where transaction processing is running, or where scanned-in data is processed. Web application servers, a new brand of Web-enabled local servers that allow for high-volume, time-critical, business-critical applications on the Web, also conceptually reside in the middle tier.
- The third tier provides the back end. This is where the corporate data warehouse, the company-wide databases, and the file system storage reside.

4.1.2 Core e-business technologies

To successfully implement e-business solutions means to put together a puzzle of different IT-technologies. While all of these technologies existed well before the advent of the Internet, they only provide their full potential in the Internet context, offering company-wide and inter-company portability and connectivity using standard Internet protocols and tools such as TCP/IP, HTTP, HTML/ XML, Java, etc.

Information retrieval

Information retrieval tools offer Boolean* search capabilities in structured and unstructured text collections. Web search engines such as AltaVista, InfoSeek, Lycos, or Excite are information retrieval tools. Vendors that existed well before the Internet such as Fulcrum or OpenText offer local or company-wide solutions as well. Document management systems (see below) generally include an information retrieval component to search the contents in their document collections.

Document management

Document management systems provide the environment for authoring, storage, and retrieval of documents. These can be simple, text-based documents, but increasingly, document management systems are also capable of handling multimedia documents containing images, audio, or video. Document management systems need to be able to distinguish between multiple versions of a document that might be accessed by different authors simultaneously. More powerful systems also handle the problem of different data formats, for example making sure that a stored WordPerfect file will still be readable in 10 or 20 years from now. Document management systems range in complexity from general-purpose tools with integrated document management capabilities such as Lotus Notes, to simple dedicated document management systems like PCDOCS, to powerful systems capable of handling hundreds of thousands of documents such as FileNet, Eastman, or Documentum. Document management systems are frequently combined with workflow management systems.

Workflow

Workflow management systems support the dynamic definition, execution, monitoring, and modification of business processes. All sorts of processes like opening a bank account, managing a supply chain, or hiring a new employee can be automated. Process control (who is doing what at what time) is separated from core business logic (such as a financial portfolio investment strategy, or accounting rules) and from data. This permits flexible adaptation of rapidly changing business processes without having to touch the other elements of the IT system. Workflow management systems are well suited to integrate existing legacy applications into new business processes. Leading workflow management systems are, for instance, Staffware, IBM's FlowMark, FileNet, and extensions of groupware system such as Lotus Notes ProzessWare. Although the concept offers striking advantages, pure workflow management solutions have had only limited success in specialized application areas. More frequently, package vendors such as SAP, PeopleSoft, Oracle, Siebel, or Ariba have integrated workflow concepts and engines into their prepackaged offerings, using the workflow component to permit custom-specific tailoring of their packages.

---

*Boolean searching uses AND, OR and NOT operators: search for a document containing "pop" AND "rock" but NOT "Michael Jackson"

Workflow management systems are typically used to send documents managed by a document management system through the organization. They are particularly well suited to support highly structured business processes. If the workflow is of an *ad hoc* nature, groupware and messaging systems are used.

Groupware/messaging

e-Mail has been one of the Internet killer applications right from its humble beginnings in the 1970s, permitting asynchronous message exchange between the academics working at the Arpanet, the predecessor of the Internet. Today's messaging products such as Microsoft Exchange and Lotus Notes offer comfortable and user friendly world-wide connectivity over the Internet. They include document management capabilities such as versioning, seamless integration of office applications like word processors and spreadsheets, multimedia integration of voice, image, and video messages, as well as workflow routing capabilities.

Just recently, dedicated fully Web-based systems for team collaboration such as eRooms, Visto, Webex, or Lotus Teamrooms have been appearing.

Data warehousing

One of the dominant features of selling goods over the Internet is mass customization. This means that customers get an automatically customized offering, based on their personal profile and preferences. Data warehousing is the enabling technology for automatic mass marketing, mining gigabytes of sales data to figure out patterns of buying behaviour. This permits vendors to come up with a personalized offering for each customer. Integrated data warehousing tools are offered by database vendors such as Oracle, dedicated high-end tools, for example from Cognos or SAS, perform complicated statistical analysis.

Web application server

Web application servers are used to link a back-end system, for instance a data warehouse, or a sales and order tracking system, with a Web front-end. Major vendors like IBM and Oracle offer their own products. There are now also at least half a dozen dedicated vendors like BlueStone, Allaire with ColdFusion, Microstate with Hamilton, and Silverstream. Web application servers work around the stateless nature of the Web. HTTP requests are stateless, which means that a Web HTTP server does not store any information about previous requests to keep a virtual connection open. Web application servers make sure that resources, including documents, user objects, and database connections persist across multiple requests to the server. Persistent database connections inherent to the Web application server engine permit applications to skip the expensive operation of connecting to a database every time a user requests a document. Web application servers connect to multiple data sources including relational databases, CICS, MQ Series, SAP, PeopleSoft, Lotus Notes, document management systems, etc. They also make Web applications suitable for enterprise deployment for tens of thousands of users, they make applications scalable by providing load-balancing features, and they improve application reliability, security and manageability. Usually, they also include utilities to create Web front-ends using both HTML and Java.

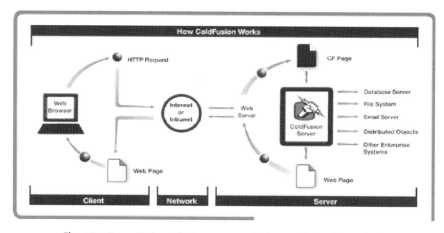

Fig. 4.2   How a Web application server works (source: Allaire Corporation).

Figure 4.2 illustrates how a Web application server works using ColdFusion:

- A Web browser requests a dynamically generated page.
- The Web HTTP server notifies the ColdFusion Web Application server.
- ColdFusion processes the dynamic page based on specific tags. If necessary, ColdFusion contacts the database, file, e-mail, or distributed object server to process the request.
- ColdFusion then dynamically generates the HTML page.
- The Web HTTP server sends the HTML page back to the browser.

Very importantly, Web application servers include object and transaction services. Thus business logic can be encapsulated in distributed middle-tier objects using standards like Microsoft COM (Component Object Model), EJB (Enterprise Java Beans) and CORBA (Common Object Request Broker Architecture). Transaction services for objects and databases can also be implemented using Web application servers.

Object-oriented middleware

Web application servers are one special type of object-oriented middleware. Depending on the needs of the applications to be integrated, other types of middleware can be used: ORBs (Object Request Brokers) such as Iona's Orbix, Microsoft's COM, or IBM's DSOM permit the integration of applications based on the OMG (Object Management Group) CORBA (Common Object Request Broker Architecture) standard. If the object request brokers communicate over the Web, a protocol called IIOP (Internet Inter-ORB Protocol) is commonly used. If reliability requirements are high, a transaction monitor guarantees fail-safe properties: A sequence of actions (the transaction) is placed between transaction brackets, assuring that the whole sequence of actions is either successfully completed, or the transaction will be reset to the original starting point in case of failure. Object request brokers and transaction monitors are currently converging: Beas' transaction monitor Tuxedo has been extended to include the CORBA object request broker protocol, while Iona's Orbix now also incorporates transaction properties.

Process-oriented packageware

Although business process automation with workflow management systems has not been a broad success so far, workflow management concepts have been integrated into leading standard software packages. These standard software packages (packageware) are moving from proprietary formats towards Internet user interfaces, standards and protocols. For example, most packages can now be accessed by Web browsers. Most business processes can be automated by packageware:

- Buying and selling: Vendors like Siebel or Vantive claim market leadership in areas such as sales force automation, call centre automation, electronic customer care, or customer relationship management.
- Design and production: ERP vendors such as SAP, PeopleSoft, or Oracle automate transaction processing in areas ranging from manufacturing to insurance. Supply chain planning and optimization is supported by tools from vendors like I2 technologies.
- Management and decision making: Controlling tools, MIS (management information systems) and data warehouses back these processes.
- Learning and change: In this area there are few pre-built packages. Learning and change processes are supported by groupware systems for collaboration such as Lotus Notes, by company-wide Intranets, and other custom-built knowledge management tools.

Java

The Java programming language has been introduced by Sun as a platform-independent Web software development environment. It has been adopted as the preferred language for developing complex Internet applications. Java applets run within the Web browser, extending its functionality by adding, for example, advanced security or animation capabilities. In the meantime, Java has grown to also become a mainstream programming language competing with languages such as C++ or Visual Basic. It is increasingly used for enterprise-wide large-scale programming projects.

4

Jini

While middleware is used to tie together applications, Sun's Jini is intended to tie together computer appliances such as printers, scanners, and PCs, but also intelligent refrigerators, and coffee machines (Fig. 4.3). Jini connection technology makes computers and devices able to quickly form spontaneously connected systems, so-called federations. Within a federation, devices are instantly on – no one needs to install them. The network is resilient – devices are simply disconnected when they are not needed. Jini technology provides simple mechanisms that enable devices to plug together to form an ad hoc community – a community put together without any planning, installation, or human intervention. Each device provides services that other devices in the community may use. Devices include their own interfaces, which ensures reliability and compatibility. Jini is fully implemented in Java. Devices in a network employing Jini technology are tied together using Java Remote

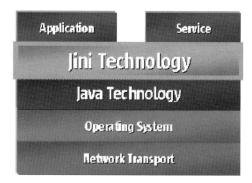

Fig. 4.3   Jini for communication between devices.

Method Invocation (RMI). Security is implemented by the built-in Java programming language security features.

Knowledge navigation and visualization

There are no ready-to-buy pre-built solutions for knowledge management and access. Instead, companies set up firm-wide Intranets and document management systems for storing knowledge. Employees are then encouraged to accumulate their explicit knowledge in structured databases, in groupware systems like Lotus Notes, or as Web documents. To access the information, customized knowledge navigation systems like InXight's Hyperbolic trees and information retrieval systems are utilized. Knowledge navigation tools and techniques are discussed in detail in Chapter 5.

Figure 4.4 combines the parts of the e-business system architecture. Object request brokers (ORBs), transaction monitors, and other middleware systems provide the glue to put together the business logic on the middle tier. Business logic applications can be grouped into knowledge management technologies such as groupware, document management, and data warehousing supporting mostly unstructured team processes. Workflow, custom-build Web applications and standard packages integrate structured business processes, normally extending over multiple teams in different parts of the company. The user

Information Visualization and Navigation					
Business Process Integration			Knowledge Navigation		
Workflow	Web Apps	Standard Packages	Groupware/ Messaging	Document Management	Data Warehousing
ORB / Transactions / Middleware / Data Bases					

Fig. 4.4   e-Business systems architecture.

interface in the first tier visualizes processes and knowledge. It should permit easy navigation between multiple applications and different knowledge bases.

The original definition language of the Web was HTML, the Hypertext Markup Language. Although it has undergone many revisions and extensions, HTML quickly reached its limit. XML, its much more powerful successor, has been designed to address all the shortcomings of HTML.

4.2 Introduction to XML

XML (eXtended Markup Language) is an extension of HTML (Hypertext Markup Language). It has been defined under the auspices of the W3 consortium with participation of prominent software companies such as Microsoft, IBM, Oracle and many more. While XML can be thought of as just a more general and complete version of a hypertext markup language, it really does much more: It makes the creation of corporate information portals much easier, it allows business intelligence to be embedded into Web applications, it enables inter-company e-commerce by substituting EDI (Electronic Data Interchange) with a standardized format, and it simplifies content management. It also assists in simpler creation of tele-learning programs, and it facilitates multi-tier Web application development, supply chain integration as well as knowledge management by providing an open and standardized format for content representation.

4.2.1 Scenarios for XML use

While HTML is a predefined set of text markup tags, XML tags can be defined by the user for each new application area. XML can thus be used in a wide range of scenarios. Because the specification of the data format can travel with the data, XML can be employed for mediation between heterogeneous databases. For example, XML-based medical information systems can easily exchange patient data, eliminating data re-entry and allowing applications to quickly note critical issues like drug allergies. XML can also be utilized for common data representations, for example as an exchange format for design tools in the semiconductor industry. Other potential uses are for presentations customized to user viewpoints, for example, showing only the sections of a multi-component manual that apply to a customer's system, or presenting one manual to a user and a different one to a system administrator. Another application area is agent-based systems, where the preferences of a particular user can be applied to the data, such as, for instance, customized TV guides that list only "interesting" shows.

4.2.2 XML basics

XML is a description format for the structure and syntax of documents based on the grandfather of page markup languages, SGML (Standardized General

Markup Language). It can be used for creating structured elements beyond those provided in HTML:

<Author>John Smith </Author>

One could create an emoticon DTD (Document Type Definition), with documents having actual

<smile>, <frown>, and <grin> tags!

This could be complemented by style sheets (including aural) which present further information on how those tags should be rendered.

(bright, loud, muted, etc.)

The big advantage compared to HTML is that XML allows the specification of new DTDs (Document Type Definitions), defining the contents and the appearance of each data element. The DTD specifications can then be attached to the data file. This means, literally speaking, that the interpreter for a language is sent along with the message. XML works like an automatically translating phone system, where an English message is translated on the fly to Japanese, because the meaning of each data element is encoded and attached to the message.

XML provides the foundation for data description and specification over the Web (Fig. 4.5). HTML can be viewed as one specific DTD of XML. Other, more specific description formats like SMIL, for multimedia, or MathML for mathematical formulas, can also be expressed in XML. Also metadata-formats, like RDF (Resource Description Format), describing the contents of a Web document in a structured way, or PICS, which allows for the selective filtering of potentially abusive contents, can be specified as XML DTDs.

The W3 consortium, the Web standards setting body, has defined the XML goals (http://www.w3.org/XML/Activity.html):

- XML should enable internationalized media-independent electronic publishing.

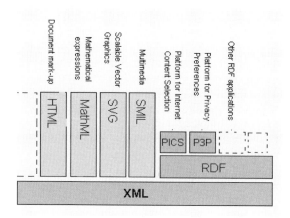

Fig. 4.5 XML as foundation of the other Web standards (source: W3 consortium).

- It should allow industries to define platform-independent protocols for the exchange of data, most importantly the data for electronic commerce.
- It should deliver information to user agents in a form that allows automatic processing after receipt.
- It should make it easy for people to process data using inexpensive software.
- It should allow people to display information the way they want it.
- It should provide metadata – data about information – that will help people find information and help information producers and consumers to find each other.

Although XML has been around for little more than a year, the computer industry, programmers, and users alike have enthusiastically embraced it. It looks well set to reach W3's ambitious goals.

4.2.3 XML features

Contrary to HTML, XML is extensible because new tags can be defined as needed. XML provides a structure that is powerful enough to model data on any level of complexity. It offers the capability to validate data by checking it for structural correctness. It is media independent, and content can be published in multiple formats. XML is also vendor and platform independent because it processes any conforming documents using standard commercial software or even simple text tools. And finally, it is broadly applicable, for example delivering information from a database to a browser.

There are already many XML-based e-commerce initiatives:

- Open Financial Exchange (http://www.ofx.net/). This is a unified specification for the electronic exchange of financial data between financial institutions, business and consumers via the Internet. Created by CheckFree, Intuit and Microsoft in early 1997, Open Financial Exchange supports a wide range of financial activities including consumer and small business banking; consumer and small business bill payment; bill presentment, and investments, including stocks, bonds and mutual funds.
- Electronic Data Exchange. The UN/EDIFACT EDI standard is currently being encoded in XML.
- Open Trading Protocol (http://www.otp.org/). The OTP group is a consortium of computer and payment systems vendors with the goal of developing standards for electronic purchasing which is independent of the chosen payment mechanism.

Other XML-based e-commerce initiatives are discussed below.

4

4.2.4 Combining XML with EDI

EDI (Electronic Data Interchange) works by providing a collection of standard message formats and an element dictionary for businesses to exchange data by an electronic messaging service. EDI uses standardized, agreed formats for electronic "messages" to create cost-efficient handling of transactions such as product re-ordering by individual shops in retail supermarket chains. EDI has been around for at least 20 years and has been used successfully by large corporations like Ford or GE to more tightly link their suppliers into their own business processes. It has also been used by financial institutions globally for interbank clearing (SWIFT/intersettle). The UN/EDIFACT standard has standardized data formats for different application areas, ranging from banking to selling the goods of developing countries by e-mail (ETO system). EDI's widespread success has been hampered for two main reasons:

- Standardization has never been sufficiently broad, always leaving too much space for interpretation for EDI software vendors. As a result, interoperability between competing EDI products is relatively poor, requiring expensive gateway products.
- EDI implementation has been very costly. EDI software products are expensive, hard to install, and in the past, run over proprietary networks such as GE's GEIS, or SWIFT.

XML now provides a standardized exchange format for workflow over the Internet. XML/EDI contributes a standard framework to exchange different types of data, for example, an invoice, or a healthcare claim, so that the information can be searched, decoded, manipulated, and displayed consistently. This information can be in a transaction, exchanged via an Application Program Interface (API), web automation, database portal, catalogue, a workflow document or an e-mail message. At first, EDI dictionaries need to be implemented, extending the vocabulary by on-line repositories to include the appropriate business language, rules and objects. There are many such EDI dictionaries under development, such as BizTalk or e-speak.

4.2.5 WebMethods Web (www.webmethods.com)

The company WebMethods uses XML to automate the exchange of data between application and legacy data sources (Fig. 4.6).

WebMethods provides the means of describing automated access to Web-enabled resources and enterprise applications through well-defined interfaces. It uses XML for bi-directional integration with ERP systems, databases, legacy systems and the Web. The ability to abstract information from Web and external application resources decreases the amount of application coding required by the developer. Also, applications are protected from changes in the original data source. WebMethod's B2B server offers templates for data formatting and transformation. The B2B Integration Server makes it possible for companies to encapsulate key business services for automated access by their trading partners. It integrates on both client and server sides with applications and business logic developed in a variety of languages and technologies such as XML, HTML, client-side Java, C/C++, Visual Basic, server-side Java, IMS, MS Excel, and other desktop applications. Server-side business logic modules can access databases, ERP applications, and EDI systems.

XML, EDI, and EDI translation servers enable companies to connect their business processes. But companies also need a way to securely transfer payments over the Web.

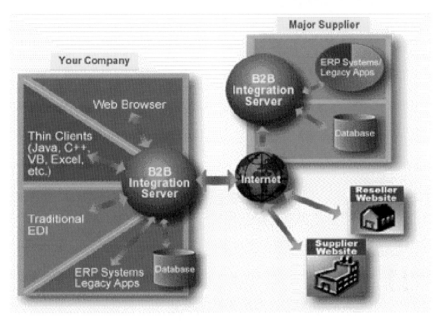

Fig. 4.6 WebMethod's B2B EDI translation server (source: WebMethods Inc.).

4.3 Security

Until very recently, Web users have been reluctant to use the Web to transfer payments. In the last year this reluctance has given way to a rapidly growing acceptance of the Web not only as an information channel, but also for buying and selling goods. Technologies available today make the Internet as secure as the phone system. Most banks today are offering electronic banking. Although there is never a 100% foolproof security system, the biggest security risks are the human users, who might forget their passwords, or give fraudulent access to their computers, or leave security codes stored on publicly accessible hard disks, etc.

To provide a secure environment for the conduct of electronic commerce over the Internet, this environment must fulfil the following three requirement:

- *Privacy*: Only the parties to a transaction should have access to the information held.
- *Authentication*: Messages are exchanged between parties whose identity has been certified by a reputable organization.
- *Non-repudiability*: A sender of a message cannot deny that they sent the message.

There are different technologies to implement these three requirements.

SSL–SHTTP

Secure Socket Layer (SSL) and Secure HTTP are Netscape's and Enterprise Integration Technology's (EIT) mechanisms to establish secure channels for communication. They are underlying frameworks for transmitting sensitive information, such as credit card numbers over the Internet. Although the use of SSL or SHTTP involves a sophisticated protocol between client and server, its application is transparent to the user. SSL creates a secure connection between a client and a server. S-HTTP transmits individual messages securely.

Digital certificates

Digital certificates are the primary means to authenticate users on the Internet. They are commonly also called "digital passports". They are issued by trusted certification authorities such as government organizations, banks, audit firms, and chambers of commerce and establish a trusted digital identity for an individual or an organization. Digital certificates are based on the ITU X.509 v3 standard for digital certificates. Leading vendors like Netscape and Microsoft use X.509 certificates to implement SSL. SSL uses a private key to encrypt data that is transferred over the SSL connection. X.509 certificates are supported both by Netscape Navigator and Internet Explorer.

Figure 4.7 illustrates what happens if Alice wants to engage in a secure Internet communication to perform, for example, Internet banking. First Alice has to request a digital certificate from a certification authority. She tells the certification authority who she is by, for example, sending her e-mail address. Depending on the level of trust and security needed, she also might have to authorize herself by making a phone call, or even go to the certification authority in person and showing some legal proof of identity. She also sends her public key to the certification authority, where it is included in her certificate. In return she gets back her digital certificate. When she then later wants to engage in e-commerce, she uses her certificate prove to the other

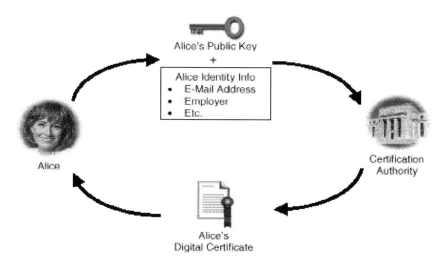

Fig. 4.7   Digital certificates.

participant that she really is Alice. To send a secure message to the other participant, she requests his certificate and uses his public key to encrypt her own message.

Despite some recent high-profile attacks on leading Web sites (e.g. Yahoo, e-Trade), the Internet can be considered safe enough to transmit an encrypted credit card number to pay for goods over the Web. Digital money has not yet reached the same level of maturity.

4.4 Digital money

There are many vendors scrambling to provide different (incompatible) variants of electronic payment schemes and digital cash over the Internet. The following listing describes current activities in this highly volatile and rapidly expanding field.

First Virtual (http://www.fv.com)

First Virtual Holdings was founded by three long-time Internet pioneers, N. Borenstein, M. Rose, and E. Stefferud. First Virtual was one of the first systems on the market. With First Virtual, the customer uses a VirtualPIN (an alias for the credit card) to make purchases. The credit card number is never transmitted over the Internet. As added security, every purchase is confirmed via e-mail: a message callback by the customer certifies the validity of a reimbursement claim of a merchant. The reimbursement is then billed to the credit card by First Virtual. In 1998 First Virtual Holdings went out of business and encouraged the customers of its Internet payment system to take their business to former competitor CyberCash.

iKP (http://www.zurich.ibm.com/Technology/Security/extern/ecommerce/iKP.html)

4

iKP (Internet keyed payment protocol) is IBM's protocol for electronic banking. It requests on-line connectivity and provides complete cryptographic protection and an audit trail. The buyer's bank account information is encrypted and then passed on to a central clearinghouse computer (preferably IBM's).

NetCash and NetCheque (http://gost.isi.edu/info/netcash/)

NetCash and NetCheque are developed by Clifford Neuman and Gennady Medvinsky at the Information Sciences Institute at the University of Southern California. NetCash is an anonymous system that provides digital coins represented as collections of bits with serial numbers that are guaranteed by a bank's signature. It requires a central computer for coin authentication. NetCheque is a non-anonymous system imitating check clearance. It uses Kerberos to generate signatures.

CheckFree (http://www.checkfree.com/)

CheckFree Corporation offers an incremental solution for moving money. The CheckFree transaction processing system was the first electronic payment system in the USA, existing before the Internet took off. A consumer can use CheckFree's software to pay monthly bills. Payments occur electronically if the merchant is wired into CheckFree's computers, otherwise CheckFree sends the merchant a paper check. CheckFree's e-bill, launched in partnership with Yahoo, is an end-to-end system for electronic billing and payment of bills over the Internet, using existing payment systems and allowing consumers to access and pay their bills through their own financial services Web site. Web BillPay is an e-bill and bill payment service. Its Express Payee list allows the user to select from predefined payees. The AutoPay feature lets them pay e-bills as presented. CheckFree is well integrated with major credit cards and the Federal Reserve Bank's electronic transfer network.

OpenMarket (http://www.openmarket.com/)

OpenMarket is a digital storefront for the secure hand-off of goods. The OpenMarket Transact server is an on-line system that checks accounts and charges before transmitting payments. TheTransact server is based on OpenMarket's SecureLink architecture which includes SecureLink commerce objects such as digital offers, coupons, receipts, tickets and queries. OpenMarket is very similar to First Virtual in that both are mere shells for exchanging funds. But contrarily to First Virtual, OpenMarket customers are charged in real-time before information is transferred to the buyer.

CyberCash (http://www.cybercash.com)

CyberCash is an on-line system with the bank acting as a third party to confirm (mostly credit card) transactions. Although it is RSA-based, it can be exported from the USA. CyberCash has provided secure credit card transactions over the Internet since April 1995. It claims to process thousands of transactions daily, have over 400,000 CyberCash Wallets in the distribution channel (including CyberCash, CheckFree, and CompuServe) and be connected to 80% of the banks in the USA.

SET

The SET protocol is a collection of encryption and security specifications used as an industry-wide standard for ensuring secure credit card payment over the Internet. It has been developed by VISA and MasterCard. The SET standard should ensure consistent implementation among vendors, card companies, and financial institutions. Furthermore, SET should establish a method for interoperability of secure transaction software over multiple hardware platforms and operating systems.

Microsoft Wallet (http://www.microsoft.com/wallet/default.asp)

Microsoft Wallet is designed for consumers and on-line businesses to make on-line shopping more convenient and secure. It allows users to store and access payment and address information. Payment information, e.g. credit cards and debit cards, is secured by password access. The Wallet is made up of

103

two parts: an address control for easily storing and retrieving ship-to and bill-to addresses, and a payment control for easily and securely storing and retrieving private payment information, such as credit cards, digital cash, electronic checks, or loyalty program data.

Microsoft TransPoint (http://www.msfdc.com/)

TransPoint is a joint venture between Microsoft, First Data Corporation (FDC), and Citibank. It offers a complete on-line bill paying service. Consumers can pay their bills on-line. Billing companies can send bills and receive payments electronically. Banks can supplement their existing offerings with on-line bill payment, alongside account balance information and financial advice. TransPoint develops the software used by billers to design custom e-bills. It also collects e-bills from billers currently within the USA at the TransPoint Service Center and consolidates the bills so consumers can receive all their e-bills in one place. It delivers the e-bills to the consumers through the Web sites of participating banks.

4.5 Virtual collaboration

In the Internet era relationships have become much closer, for example changing "customer–vendor" relationships into true partnerships. The Internet provides the perfect communication mechanism to support virtual teams spanning the globe. Although there are situations where there is no replacement for face-to-face communication, Web-based communication technologies make it much easier for physically separated teams to work together, dramatically reducing the need for face to face meetings.

Lotus Notes has defined the domain of groupware systems for collaboration. Notes/Domino, now under IBM's ownership, is still one of the leading products in this area, although Microsoft with its Exchange/Outlook product is close on its heels. Both Notes/Domino and Exchange/Outlook are extended e-mail systems, which are in their current versions almost seamlessly integrated into the Web. Because of their upbringing, they still do have some fundamental differences. The Notes package excels in the replication of unstructured or semi-structured databases. It also contains an integrated programming environment supporting three different programming languages: a macro language, a scripting language called LotusScript, and Java.

Microsoft Exchange grew out of Microsoft Mail and still is message based. Replication functionality is by now also included, this is particularly useful for mobile users and workgroups that can replicate and share mailboxes and other files. Contrary to Notes, programming capabilities are not built into Exchange, but extended customizing needs to be done using other Microsoft development tools such as Access, Excel, Visual Basic, Visual C++, or Visual Java.

4

4.5.1 Virtual Workgroups

Virtual workgroups can be supported by setting up a work environment in Notes or Exchange, possibly connected by the Internet. Nevertheless, implementing a workgroup system in Notes or Exchange still involves a substantial amount of customization and even application development. There are now at least a dozen vendors that have recognized this need and are offering out-of-the-box software for virtual workgroups, based on the Internet. The following listing of vendors is by no means final:

- eRoom (www.eroom.com)
- Webex (www.webex.com)
- Visto (www.visto.com)
- Instant!Teamroom (www.lotus.com/home.nsf/tabs/teamroom)
- Sametime (www.lotus.com/home.nsf/tabs/sametime)
- Teamspace (www.involv.com)
- Groupsystems (www.ventana.com)
- www.teamsoft.com
- www.projectplace.com
- www.anexa.com

eRoom

eRoom is one of the leaders in this field. It provides an on-line virtual out-of-the-box project office. Web pages are either hosted on eRoom's servers; alternatively, the software can be run on the firm-internal Intranet of the client company.

Figure 4.8 displays the typical work environment of a member of a team working with eRoom. eRoom's desktop displays a shared project space, where team members can communicate in real-time, but also share all sorts of thoughts and documents. eRoom offers drag-and-drop folders, where a file can be

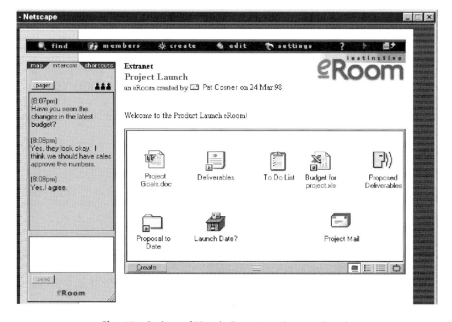

Fig. 4.8 Desktop of Virtual eRoom team (source: eRoom).

grabbed from the Windows desktop and made accessible to the team member by dragging it with the mouse into a shared folder. There is a sophisticated mechanism to define different levels of membership. Group tasks can be managed by creating structured "to do lists". eRroom supports taking polls, to resolve open group issues. Web links can be shared in special "link" documents. There are also useful document management features, such as tracking multiple versions of a document, or controlling access to documents. To support navigation in shared project spaces, maps of projects can be created (Fig. 4.9).

The left window in Fig. 4.8 illustrates real-time communication between team members in an intercom chat window. To find information in complex project spaces, search functions to search all documents in the global project space are provided.

Webex (http://www.webex.com)

The Webex system is very similar to eRooms. It allows for virtual meetings, offices, and project suites that are shared over the Web. A group of users can establish group identity. Members of the group can create multiple offices with a consistent look. They can invite private guest attendees, share a group calendar, participate in discussion forums, and also send inter-group messages. Webex facilitates application sharing.

Visto (http://www.visto.com)

The Visto product consists of three parts: My Visto, My Groups, and My Events. My Visto contains a calendar, e-mail, address book and file storage service. My Groups lets the user create multiple interactive groups, where

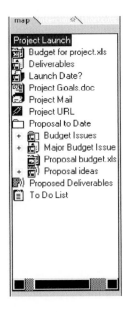

Fig. 4.9   Project map (source: eRoom).

family, friends, and colleagues can interact, share photos and files and plan events. My Events gives the user easy access to event listings in different categories. Events can be selected and tracked on the calendar.

Instant!Teamroom and Sametime

Lotus offers two Notes-based systems for team collaboration. Instant!Team-room (Www.lotus.com/home.nsf/tabs/teamroom) allows users to set up a private workspace on the Web (see Fig. 4.10). It uses a Notes Domino server to implement this functionality.

Sametime (http://www.lotus.com/home.nsf/tabs/sametime) (Fig. 4.11) helps business users to communicate with colleagues, partners and customers. It provides chat, audioconferencing, shared whiteboards and shared applications. Users can find co-workers on-line, chat with them instantaneously, and share documents to simultaneously work on them.

Teamspace (http://www.involv.com)

Teamspace is yet another system for project collaboration. It includes document management capabilities, group discussion support, a shared group calendar, chat and paging functions, issue management, a bulletin board, and an event and meeting planner. A distinctive feature of Teamspace is its virtual classroom for group training.

GroupSystems (http://www.ventana.com)

Contrary to the other systems described in this section, GroupSystems not only embodies a Web-based system for virtual cooperation, but also includes a methodology. The methodology consists of four steps:

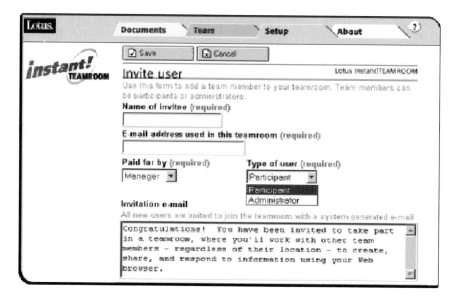

Fig. 4.10   Lotus Instant!Teamroom workspace (source: Lotus Development Corporation).

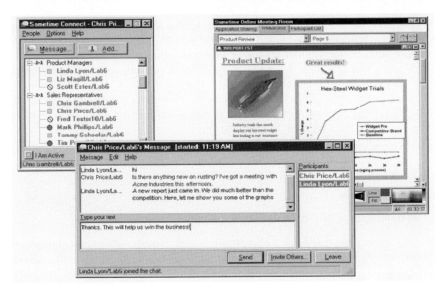

Fig. 4.11   Lotus Sametime (source: Lotus Development Corporation).

(1) Set a clear agenda.
(2) Let everyone speak at once.
(3) Analyze and explore the issues.
(4) Develop consensus and buy-in.

   The common characteristic of the above listed software systems for virtual workgroups is that all the functions needed to support group activities are already built-in. In contrast, when solely using Lotus Notes or Microsoft Exchange, these functions must be implemented first. This makes Notes and Exchange potentially more powerful, but also much harder to install. More specifically, to set up a Notes- or Exchange-based collaboration system, good systems management and programming skills are mandatory.

   If different authors want to edit the same document simultaneously over the Web, they need applications that support contemporary authoring. The WebDAV standard makes sure that different applications from different vendors support this functionality.

4.5.2 WebDAV

The Internet standards-setting community has defined the WebDAV (www.webdav.org) standard for distributed authoring and versioning. The charter document at www.ietf.org/html.charters/webdav-charter.html describes WebDAV's goals. Microsoft is throwing its weight behind WebDAV, including WebDAV support in its newest version of the Internet Explorer, and promising WebDAV support in the next versions of Microsoft Office and Information Server. Besides many public domain and shareware products, there are already commercial WebDAV servers from Xerox, Glyphica, and DMC.

WebDAV defines HTTP extensions to enable distributed Web authoring tools to be interoperable. WebDAV standards include services such as file locking, versioning, the definition of properties for improved searching, and namespace manipulation for remote operations such as copying, moving of files, or grouping of files into collections. WebDAV uses XML to allow clients to make property queries. WebDAV can be viewed as a network filesystem suitable for the Internet. It provides a protocol for manipulating the contents of a document management system via the Web.

"HTTP gives read access, while WebDAV gives write access to Web files".

4.6 Workflow management

Rising costs, international competition, and rapidly changing boundary conditions require fast and flexible adaptation to a quickly evolving business environment. While earlier improvement efforts left the internal business organization intact, business process reengineering (BPR) (Hammer and Champy, 1992) places its whole emphasis on rebuilding the corporation. As enabling technology for BPR, workflow management has become increasingly popular in the last few years. Workflow management deals with the specification and execution of business processes. A workflow management system provides the responsible person with the relevant activity and the necessary data at the right point in the process. General workflow specifications include the actions to be performed, routing information and policies that describe the organizational environment. By computationally supporting business processes, workflow management systems reduce reaction time to changing requirements and to the emergence of new organizational concepts. Workflow management systems allow one to dynamically define, execute, manage, and modify business processes. It is irrelevant whether these are business-critical processes such as opening a bank account, buying insurance, applying for credit, or company-internal processes such as job applications or procurement of new office supplies.

4.6.1 Basic concepts

Each workflow management project has three dimensions (Fig. 4.12):

(1) Process view: The formalized description of the business process is the basis for the computerized support of this process. The description can be given as a flow chart, as a table, or as a formalized description in a specification language.
(2) Organization view: Each step in the process, i.e. each activity, is executed by some actors. These actors assume a particular role in that activity, e.g. accountant, supervisor, customer, etc.
(3) IT view: The workflow engine controls the process flow. It connects the screen forms needed to input and output data on each process step, and the worklist listing the "to do" items for the person participating in the process. The workflow engine also might connect other external

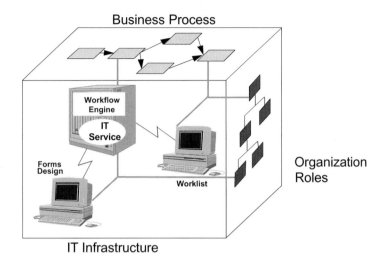

Fig. 4.12 Three dimensions of workflow management.

applications such as an accounting module, a spreadsheet, or an investment strategy application which exchange data with the workflow process, but are not directly part of the process.

Figure 4.13 displays a sample workflow process. A customer is applying for a new health insurance policy. He first enters his personal information on a form (1). The form is then examined from the medical perspective, and if there are no hidden risks discovered, the premium is computed automatically, the policy printed and mailed to the customer. If the customer data reveals hidden risks, the customer is invited to a medical examination to a health care centre (2). There he is examined (3), the doctor enters the customer data into a form (4), a

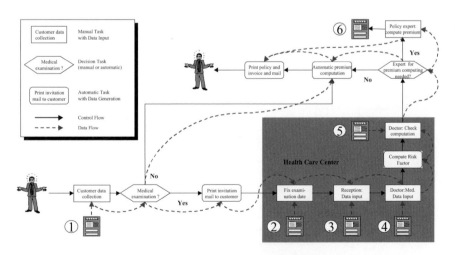

Fig. 4.13 Sample workflow process: health insurance.

risk factor is computed, and the results (5) are sent to a health insurance expert. The expert might then compute the premium manually (6).

Note that at this level of detail there are no assumptions about what process steps might be automated using a computer. The sample process works independently whether all the data forwarding is done using paper forms, the data is forwarded from one process step to the next using e-mail, or a fully integrated workflow management system is used.

4.6.2 The Workflow Management Coalition (WfMC)

From a software engineering perspective, workflow management systems are particularly attractive. Using a workflow management system isolates the control flow of an application from the domain-specific business logic. Permanent data and operations on this data, such as accounting, are much more stable than the business process itself. By logically separating the process control flow from the data, it is much easier to modify the business process without having to change the application and data structure. Workflow management systems are also particularly well suited for the integration of existing application modules into new applications. This makes it much simpler to reengineer legacy applications so that old and new application components can be easily integrated.

For widespread acceptance of workflow management systems, particularly between different companies, adherence to interface standards is of paramount importance. While the Workflow Management Coalition (WfMC) reference model (Fig. 4.14) tries to define a general framework, the reference model still falls short of assuring interoperability between different workflow management systems.

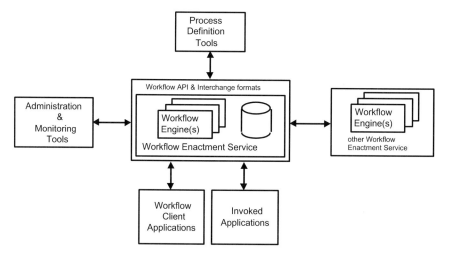

Fig. 4.14 WfMC reference model (Workflow Management Coalition, 1995).

4.6.3 SWAP (Simple Workflow Access Protocol) (www.ics.uci.edu/~ietfswap)

Most workflow vendors today persue a different approach to assure interoperability between different workflow engines by using Web standards such as HTML or XML as the least common denominator. Unfortunately, Web integration is mostly limited to offering a web browser interface to different proprietary workflow engines. Very recently, a more open approach has been pursued by using portable Web technology not only as a front-end for the workflow client applications, but also for the implementation of the workflow enactment service and for administration and monitoring.

The IETF (Internet Engineering Task Force), the main standards body of the Internet community, has set up the SWAP working group (Simple Workflow Access Protocol). The goal of the SWAP working group is to assure interoperability between different workflow systems by defining a common protocol. Contrary to WfMC and the OMG (Object Management Group), yet another standards body also active in the workflow area, SWAP's approach is based on HTTP. It is less ambitious than WfMC and OMG, but might have a better chance to achieve its goals. SWAP is currently working on an application level Workflow Interoperability protocol, where notification and transaction control is added. All parameters are put into XML encoding to be sent with the appropriate calls. Wherever possible, other already available Internet standards are used. For assigning and retrieving properties of a resource, the WebDAV standard described above is used.

Standards like SWAP are particularly valuable for automating processes spanning company boundaries, where different workflow engines need to talk to each other. The Internet protocols and standards provide the least common denominator.

4.6.4 Problems with the current generation of workflow systems

Although workflow management systems still have a long way to go until they can be considered a mature technology, the first generation of commercial systems has started to find some acceptance. To name a few, systems such as FileNet, IBM FlowMark, Action Technology Action Workflow System, Staffware, and Eastman OPEN/Workflow offer usable solutions today. Nevertheless, all of these commercially available systems exhibit some common weaknesses. Dedicated special-purpose workflow systems lack transactional properties that are commonplace in database systems. Features such as concurrence, high availability, performance, scalability, and fault-tolerance are an integral part of transaction monitors, but not of workflow engines. There are additional problems inherent in the nature of workflow systems:

- Extendibility: A few systems such as DEC Linkworks (Digital Equipment, 1995) allow the user to dynamically modify a particular process instance by rerouting the work item in the worklist to additional users. But most workflow systems are currently limited to executing canned processes that have been previously defined and are stored in the internal process database of the workflow enactment engine.

- Flexible organization structure: Current workflow systems have a built-in database of the organizational structure that defines the recipients for each work item. This mechanism does not scale well for large workflows in large organizations. It is also hard to keep up-to-date for rapidly changing processes and organizations. There have been some solutions proposed, most prominently language-based approaches such as the one by DEC (Bush, 1994). Unfortunately, most of these approaches currently exist only on paper.

- Structured and unstructured processes: Workflow systems are well suited to support structured processes (Fig. 4.15). Unfortunately, complex real-world processes frequently have an unstructured as well as a structured part. For example, a "new product approval process" consists of informally collecting opinions of colleagues as well as a predefined approval process within the company hierarchy. Commercial workflow systems are poorly equipped for handling such semi-structured processes. IBM offers a possible solution by combining its workflow system FlowMark with the groupware system Lotus Notes. Obviously this approach provides only the technological infrastructure; it is still up to the workflow programmer to implement interfaces to unstructured workflows.

Workflow management offers a great concept. Unfortunately, until now, the great breakthrough has not yet happened. The market is heavily fragmented with dozens of vendors, the distinction between workflow, groupware, and document management is blurred and adds to the confusion. In the standardization area, there is competition between three standards bodies: WfMC, IETF SWAP, and OMG. While the WfMC standard has progressed the most, (it also has been around the longest), commitment and support from major players such as Microsoft, IBM, Netscape, Oracle, and FileNet, while

	Workgroup	Workflow
Process Type	unstructured (ad-hoc) processes	structured processes
	support of teamwork	productive business processes
Number of Participants per Process	"short" processes in small team	company-wide
	few participants per process	many different participants
User Interaction	Users decide when and what information they want to receive	Users are presented with information on which they have to make decisions
Emphasis	Sharing Information	Routing Information

Fig. 4.15　Workgroup and workflow processing.

verbally given, have been less than forthcoming. No major player so far has moved aggressively into the driver's seat. Rather, competition and the desire to convert its own product features to standards have made the standards-setting process slow and tedious. On the technical side, the transaction property still does not fully work for workflow management systems. To obtain high reliability all of the vendors suggest combining their workflow product with a transaction monitor. IBM has even integrated FlowMark into its message queuing product MQ/Series.

4.6.5 The future: Workflow by packageware?

Workflow management systems are certainly suited for well-structured processes, where clearly defined rules determine the execution order of the process steps. Unstructured processes are better supported by groupware systems. These are processes where people cooperate on an *ad hoc* basis, which is frequently the case in the new product creation process or in project management processes.

In the last few years, however, we have seen a growing tendency towards packageware. Systems in areas ranging from ERP and sales and marketing to procurement are supported by systems from vendors like SAP, Siebel, or Ariba. Processes in the upper-right quadrant of Fig. 4.16, automated production processes, are particularly well suited for this approach. These software packages automate generic versions of the business processes, often internally using a workflow engine for process customization, control and automation.

4.7 Business process integration

In recent years we have seen a growing tendency towards seamless integration of business processes. Information technology and the Internet play a crucial role here. Global companies use the Intranet or Extranet to communicate internally using Internet technologies. But the integration of business

4

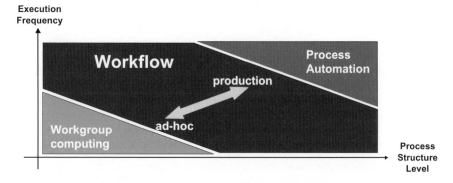

Fig. 4.16. From groupware to workflow to process automation.

processes does not stop at company boundaries. Supply chain processes are integrated using the Web and other e-commerce technologies from the supplier through the producer to the consumer. Customers can now be integrated into product development processes in ways that were never considered a few years ago. Just think about software development, where customers voluntarily assume the roles of software beta testers. Other examples abound, ranging from inventory management, where a supplier manages the warehouse of its customer, to logistics and transportation, which today is frequently outsourced to specialized companies like UPS or FedEx, to helpdesk services, where company-internal IT support is provided by specialized companies using sophisticated call centre software.

The trend goes towards integrating all crucial business processes:

- Buying and selling: e-business technologies support all aspects of the selling process: sales force automation (SFA) and electronic customer care (ECC) tools help sales staff manage addresses and correspondence of customers and prospects. They assist not only in the planning of mass mailings and marketing campaigns, but also in integrating multimedia product presentations. In addition, some tools help in the creation of sales configuration systems, where a prospective customer can create a virtual configuration of a complex product, such as an offset printing press, to explore pricing and configuration options.

- Design and production: This is the classic domain of ERP tools, which automate all the internal design, production and manufacturing processes. ERP tools also support financial and management accounting, as well as human resource administration. Relative newcomers to this field extend their reach into areas such as procurement over the Internet, or supply chain planning and optimization.

- Management and decision making: Management information systems sit on top of financial and accounting systems and deliver condensed management information to the executive. Data warehouses collect information from different databases. From there, all sorts of evaluations and reports can be produced using drill-down and other analytical and statistic technologies. Results are, for example, used to discover buying patterns in large amounts of customer data or to make recommendations to a customer based on previous buying behaviour. The management should change from a reactive mode of decision making to trying to "anticipate the future".

- Learning and change: In this area there are few out-of-the-box solutions. Lotus Notes is considered a knowledge management tool. There are also multimedia authoring systems to create computer-based training courses. Change management can be supported by Lotus Notes-based applications. The common characteristic of tools in this area is that they have little incorporated process knowledge. Rather, these tools are programming environments where each application is custom-built from scratch. The next chapter describes general concepts and principles for the construction of such knowledge management applications.

To link business processes, the underlying IT systems needs the capability to link information seamlessly and automatically. Normally, a logical hub is implemented that directs the flow of information throughout the enterprise.

This can be a middleware product such as an object request broker, a transaction monitor, or a workflow management system. The built-in workflow system of ERP systems like SAP, Peoplesoft, or Baan can also assume this role. The logical hub needs to support many-to-many application connections and intelligent message flow based on business rules. These business rules are either built into the ERP system, or programmed out for the object request broker or transaction monitor, or specified as flowcharts for a workflow management system. A messaging system like Exchange or Notes acts as a "message warehouse" or information store. Alternatively, under special circumstances, the built-in messaging system of the ERP system can be used. Finally, the logical hub needs to support a wide range of platforms and formatting standards including XML.

From middleware to packageware

There are different middleware products available, acting as "glue" to integrate heterogeneous systems. The middleware products are based on distinct principles, metaphors, and technologies. They have taken steps in very different directions.

Operating systems such as Microsoft Windows and NT, or Unix in derivatives such as Sun Solaris, Linux, or HP/UX all include middleware capabilities. Microsoft has established itself as the de facto standard on the desktop side, and also has the greatest number of installed NT servers, which makes Microsoft DCOM an obvious choice for communication in pure Microsoft networks.

In the relational database world, Oracle is the undisputed leader, while Microsoft SQL Server offers a low-end entry for mid-sized databases running on NT networks. To integrate products at the database level, a company is well advised to standardize on one product to solve their portability and integration chores.

For the "real" middleware products, the choice is not so easy. Transaction monitors and message queuing systems have found practical use in specialized areas, where fault-tolerance and high reliability of transactions are imperative. Products from Bea (Tuxedo), Microsoft (Transaction Server), IBM (MQ/Series), etc. are in use. As long as a company standardizes on one product, integration is feasible with reasonable effort. Unfortunately, in practice, this is not so easy, because middleware from big operating system vendors tends to work well with their vendor's system, but not so well with other vendor's operating system. For example, MQ/Series and CICS are tuned to work well in an IBM environment, while Microsoft's Transaction Server and Message Queuing server run primarily on Windows and NT. Products from independent middleware vendors such as Bea's Tuxedo, pursue a more open approach. Unfortunately, this "one-size-fits-many" approach also means that deploying these systems on the different operating platforms can be more cumbersome than the native product of the operating system vendor.

CORBA (Common Object Request Broker Architecture) of the OMG (Object Management Group) has addressed this problem by trying to define a universal middleware standard. In theory, object brokers from different vendors should all be interoperable as long as they use the CORBA standard. In practice, though, each vendor has interpreted the standard differently and also added its own features, with the result that full interoperability between different object brokers is non-existent. Because there is no clear leader in this field, companies should choose the object broker that works best within their local system environment.

Convergence between transaction monitors and object brokers is already taking place. Transaction monitor vendors such as Bea are integrating object brokers while object broker vendors like Iona are adding transaction monitor capabilities. For example, Bea's latest offering will support both the Common Object Request Broker Architecture (CORBA) and Microsoft's Distributed Component Object Model (DCOM). The underpinnings of the Bea engine are the Tuxedo transaction monitor, and ObjectBroker, an Object Request Broker that Bea acquired from Digital Equipment Corp. in 1996.

Workflow management systems, described in the previous section, would provide a compelling solution, combining the best of all worlds of business process control and integration, transaction monitors, and object brokers. Unfortunately, although the concept was greeted enthusiastically by customers and analysts alike some 5 years ago, the breakthrough has yet to come.

Workflow concepts have made their inroads in software packages. All integrated packages automate business processes by managing the workflow, be it enterprise resource planning where SAP is the clear leader, or customer relationship management, where the leading vendor Siebel has equally embraced the workflow concept. Similarly, call centres have been automated using workflow concepts by vendors such as Vantive, while procurement workflows are supported by operating resources management systems from Ariba or Commerce One.

4.7.1 ERP integration

Enterprise resource planning systems have become ubiquitous in the corporate world. They provide predefined solutions in areas such as accounting and controlling, production and materials management, quality management and plant maintenance, and human resources management. Leading vendors for large companies are SAP, Peoplesoft, Oracle, Baan, and J.D. Edwards. SAP, based in Walldorf, Germany, is by far the largest ERP vendor. We will limit our discussion here to SAP's system and its e-business strategy; systems and strategies of its competitors are similar.

SAP and mySAP.com

SAP is the undisputed leader in the ERP market. With its mySAP.com initiative, it is now also moving quickly into the e-business area, combining SAP's business applications with standard Internet technologies. R/3, the current version of SAP's business applications, is based on relational databases and three-tier client/server technology. At R/3's core are programs for accounting and controlling, production and materials management, quality management and plant maintenance, sales and distribution, human resources management, and project management. Information and early warning systems are also available. The Business Information Warehouse is composed of external and internal data to support decision-making at all corporate levels.

Although designed as an integrated system, SAP R/3's modules can also be used individually. Sales and materials planning, production planning, warehouse management, financial accounting, and human resources management are integrated into a workflow of business events and processes across departments and functional areas. The goal is to assure that employees receive the right information and documents at the right time at their desktops. Corporate headquarters, manufacturing plants, sales offices, and subsidiaries all merge for integrated handling of business processes.

SAP R/3 already provides business process integration over company boundaries in its native version – as long as all involved parties are using a SAP R/3 system. Its applications link a company's business processes with those of customers and suppliers to create complete logistical chains covering the entire route from supply to delivery. SAP R/3 lets one integrate banks and other business partners into intercompany communications, both nationally and internationally. Of course, direct seamless integration only works if all companies involved run the SAP R/3 system.

SAP R/3 has integrated the business processes in an overall system for planning, controlling and monitoring. A client company can currently choose from about 800 ready-made business processes. They include best business practices across various industries.

SAP has partnered with other industry heavyweights to define its e-business initiative mySAP.com: IBM provides Internet technology, the Microsoft BizTalk Framework is used for electronic data interchange, and on-line malls from Intershop and Pandesic are integrated. AT&T and Deutsche Telekom grant Internet access; webMethod's XML technology, Inktomi's search engine and Tibco's middleware provide the software building blocks.

The mySAP.com package (Fig. 4.17) is comprised of four key elements; mySAP-Employee Workplace, a personalized, role-based user interface; mySAP.Business Scenarios, products for the Internet and Intranet; the SAP portal www.mySAP.com; and SAP applications hosted on the Web.

With the new personalized role-based user interface "mySAP-Employee Workplace", employees get role-specific services and scenarios, single sign-on and server-based user profiles, and personalization and simplification capabilities. Employee Workplace extends documents with context-sensitivity for business data and transactions. mySAP.Business Scenarios are functional subsets of multiple products tailored to specific roles within an organization. They include SAP Business-to-Business Procurement, SAP Business-to-Business Selling, SAP Business-to-Consumer and enhanced SAP Employee Self Service. In addition, SAP intends to provide services via the mySAP.com portal. The portal is comprised of software, services, information content and Web infrastructure technology. Specifically, the SAP portal offers individuals industry-specific, cross-industry and private services for work, market and home. mySAP.com also includes third-party products and services, creating an "Internet marketplace for cooperation, electronic trading and commerce".

mySAP.com is targeting small and mid-size companies with Web-based application hosting services, to offer a cost-effective approach for companies to use SAP Business Scenarios and to engage in Internet collaborative markets. Application hosting is also intended to provide the opportunity to companies to implement SAP solutions adjacent to each other or even on the same database, enabling direct inter-enterprise business collaboration.

4

Fig. 4.17   mySAP.com strategy (source: SAP).

SAP wants to provide Web access to all SAP R/3 modules and to deliver Web-based business scenarios to customers in areas such as supply chain planning, customer relationship management and business intelligence.

4.7.2 Supply chain planning

While the actual management and handling of the company-internal supply chain is the realm of SAP and its ERP siblings, there are other systems dedicated to optimizing the supply chain along the whole lifecycle of a product.

I2 Technologies (I2 www.i2.com) positions itself as the inventor of electronic business process optimization. I2 wants to enable its customers to give to consumers "the right product at the right time, at the right price, and at the right place".

To plan and optimize the supply chain, I2 offers three main modules:

- *Demand Fulfilment* is intended to provide fast, accurate, and reliable delivery-date responses to customer orders.
- *Demand Planning* should enable its users to understand their customers' buying patterns and develop aggregate, collaborative forecasts.
- *Supply Planning* should position enterprise resources to meet the demand.

Besides supply chain planning, I2 offers other functionality such as the Product Lifecycle Management module that uses planning and optimization methods to address the entire product lifecycle – from concept, development, test, to launch and phase out. Its goal is to maximize the speed, productivity, market-share capture, and financial return of the product development process. In addition, I2 includes a strategic planning module delivering scenario-based simulations of current and future business conditions to better understand the strengths and weaknesses of competitors. I2 offers off-the-shelf adapters to third party ERP, customer relationship management (CRM), and other systems providing both process flow and data flow integration.

ERP systems try to fully automate the supply chain. Supply chain planning systems try to optimize the supply chain. But there is another huge flow of money and goods between companies that is not directly product-related. Ariba and Commerce One have pioneered what its called e-procurement, the corporate buying of non-production goods and services.

4.7.3 e-Procurement with Ariba

Ariba, a recent Internet startup, provides e-procurement services primarily to the global Fortune 2000 companies. Similarly to its competitor Commerce One, Ariba is a leading provider of so-called ORMS (operating resources management systems): Operating resources are the non-production goods and services that businesses acquire and manage to run their day-to-day business operations. They include services, capital equipment, maintenance, repair, and operating (MRO) supplies, travel and entertainment, and other items requiring approvals through internal business processes. For example, communications and computer equipment, software, advertising and corporate expenses, industrial and office supplies, travel and entertainment expenses, facilities and services, and scientific and industrial supplies are all operating resources. Ariba's goal is that every employee of an Ariba client company has the buying applet on her PC, and buys all the goods directly online (Fig. 4.18).

Ariba business model

I had the chance to get an inside view at Ariba, to learn about its product strategy, and to see how its software is being developed. My conclusion is that

4

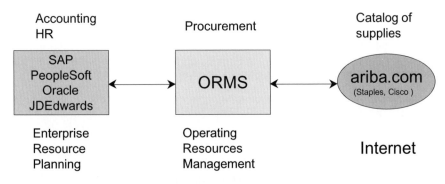

Fig. 4.18 Ariba ORMS.

its success can be attributed primarily to general principles of good management.

- *Stick to core competencies:* Ariba currently exclusively positions its software for operating resources management, and withstands the temptation to extend its software package with other functionality, for example, to also include functions for the procurement of the raw materials of a manufacturing company. In particular, Ariba ORMS currently is not a production and planning systems (PPS).
- *Sound, reliable product:* The Ariba ORMS system has an extremely easy-to-use interface that can be used without end-user training. The back-end system is simple and stable, the required transaction properties are derived from the underlying databases. For the implementation of the Ariba server, pragmatic decisions were taken that can be changed if the environment changes. For the data exchange format, it was decided to initially use a proprietary format and to change it if compelling business reason would make it necessary. In particular, neither an EDI/EDIFACT standard nor the Process Interchange Format (PIF) of the Workflow Management Coalition (WfMC) were used. Similarly, the communication protocol sits directly on TCP/IP sockets; neither CORBA nor RMI were used primarily because when Ariba development started neither was available in a sufficiently stable format. Product catalogues are replicated into the ORMS database, Ariba is using its own Catalog Interchange Format (CIF), which allows a supplier to export its product catalogue as a flat file for import into the ORMS database.
- *Good product strategy and marketing:* Ariba initially sees the Fortune 2000 companies as its main customers, wanting to put the Ariba ORMS applet on every desktop of their hundred thousands of employees. The Fortune 2000 companies also have pockets which are deep enough to invest the millions needed for company-wide deployment of an ORMS. This gives Ariba a sound initial revenue stream for further product development. The combined buying power of the Ariba corporate customers (hundreds of billions of US dollars) makes it attractive for suppliers to have their product catalogues available in ORMS format.

The second product of Ariba, ariba.com, is an Internet corporate procurement marketplace (Fig. 4.19). With ariba.com, Ariba is moving from selling software to providing services. Ariba.com, a secure Web site, is intended to more easily link users of Ariba's business-to-business purchasing application to their suppliers. Ariba.com routes purchase transactions entered into the ORMS directly to selected suppliers' electronic catalogues. Suppliers can also send customized pricing and product updates directly to buyers. Ariba intends to pioneer seamless integration of payment services by centralized clearing and logistics.

Ariba is taking a somewhat reluctant stance towards standardization, it is not actively participating in the relevant standard setting bodies such as ISO (International Standards Organization) for EDIFACT, OMG (Object Management Group) for CORBA, or WfCM (Workflow Management Coalition) for workflow definition. Rather, it is pursuing the Microsoft approach by letting the market accept a proprietary format (preferably its own) as a de facto standard.

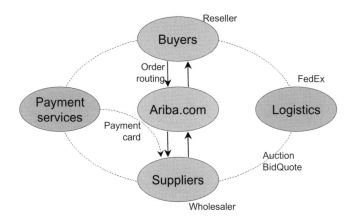

Fig. 4.19 Ariba.com business model.

On the other hand, Ariba is actively pushing an XML-based description standard for buying and selling goods over the Web: Commerce XML (cXML), a new set of document type definitions (DTDs) for XML. cXML is an explicit meta-language to describe the characteristics of items available for sale. It enables the development of "intelligent shopping agents" that help to do the work of corporate purchasing. By programming the characteristics that a buyer is seeking into request messages and releasing them to the network, the request supposedly returns exactly what the buyer is seeking or nothing at all – which in itself is sometimes important to know. Ariba compares cXML to "bar coding" for the Web, but with a richer set of attributes to uniquely identify and describe products, which can be incorporated into computer programs.

Ariba does not only automate existing procurement processes, but has fundamentally reengineered the way in which procurement is done.

4.7.4 Customer relationship management with Siebel

In the same way that Ariba revolutionized the procurement area, Siebel has fundamentally changed the way in which all activities around customer care are being performed. It has defined a new class of Web-based systems called "customer relationship management" systems. Similarly to SAP, the Siebel system consists of different modules in areas ranging from e-business, sales, service, call centre, field service, and marketing to product configuration. Siebel is complex to configure and install in a similar way to SAP, requiring skilled consultants and programmers experienced in business analysis, Internet technologies, and large-scale project management.

Siebel's Web-based architecture supports global organizations, scaling to create sales, marketing and customer service solutions that meet the needs of the entire corporation. Siebel claims high-performance support for thousands of mobile, connected, and Internet-based users working with terabytes of data. It allows mobile users to synchronize their changes with those made on their regional or corporate server by delivering only the updated information to the mobile user. The Siebel applications allow sales, marketing, and service organizations to transact business in multiple time zones with automatic conversion of quotes and forecasts into a single, common currency. Siebel communicates with external applications via COM and CORBA interfaces. It offers a workflow manager for organizations to model and automate their specific policies and procedures throughout sales, marketing, and customer service. In call centres, Siebel supports "intelligent" call routing and call handling to ensure that the customer interacts with the sales or service agent best qualified to serve the customer. It includes a scripting system called "SmartScript" to help employees manage their workflow with dynamically generated scripting.

The sales module claims to make sales professionals "significantly more effective", helping them increase the probability of winning a deal, shortening the sales cycle, and increasing the value of each transaction. The sales module includes opportunity and sales pipeline management, profile and account management, a multi-media, Web-enabled marketing encyclopaedia with information about products and pricing, competitors, decision issues, objection handling tools, and complete sales tools including brochures, data sheets, presentations, and videos. It offers integrated correspondence and fulfilment, instant and assisted quote generation, one-button customized proposals, and automatic sales presentations.

Besides Siebel, there are other specialized software vendors in this area like Vantive, Trilogy, or Broadvision. ERP vendors like SAP or Peoplesoft are also adding customer relationship management capability to their systems. And at the lower end, on-line shopping mall software vendors are also including some of these functions into their products.

4.7.5 On-line shopping malls

On-line shopping malls are on the other end of the spectrum of customer relationship management: they set up a virtual storefront, where the end-user can directly buy goods. While Siebel-like systems take care of all facets of the customer, on-line shopping malls focus on the selling aspect. Initially, the greatest potential of e-commerce has been seen in this area: billions of customers connected to the Web, shopping around the globe in one virtual marketplace, happily buying goods from anywhere in the world. In the meantime, enthusiasm in this business-to-consumer-field has cooled off somewhat, particularly after analysts like Gartner Group, Forrester Research, and Giga Group have declared the business-to-business e-commerce domain to have the greatest growth potential and profit margin. Systems like SAP, I2, Ariba, and Siebel cater to this clientele.

Nevertheless, there are still numerous virtual storefronts, be it as extensions of "real" businesses, like the web bookstore barnesandnoble.com, or as purely virtual business, with no physical store, like Amazon.com. The growth potential in this area is still enormous with every computer-owner linked to the Internet being a virtual customer. And in the USA well above 40% of all households now own a computer, with European and Asian countries picking up on Internet penetration.

Major software vendors have their own on-line shopping mall systems. IBM Net.Commerce, Microsoft Site Server Commerce Edition, Lotus Domino. Merchant, Netscape MerchantXpert all allow companies to set up a virtual storefront. There are also specialized vendors like BroadVision and Brokat for the finance industry, while some of the biggest on-line vendors like Amazon are developing their own, custom-built virtual stores.

Internet shopping malls exhibit common characteristics (Fig. 4.20). They all provide some sort of interface to set up a virtual storefront to display the goods on the Internet. Not all of them are as fancy as the three-dimensional virtual world in the virtual mall of ActiveWorlds, where the customer can assume a virtual identity, and then see a picture of his alter ego, walking around in the mall, entering stores, or looking at the items on display (Fig. 4.21). The second part of the Internet shopping mall is a virtual shopping cart, where a customer can add items from the selection, or put them back onto the virtual shelf. The third part is a product search and selection module, where users can easily locate the goods they are looking for. Good product searching functions are absolutely essential, because the flashiest GUI and the best products on sale are useless if a customer can not find them. The quality of the user-specific predefined selections is dependent on the quality of the middle-tier user profiling and data warehousing modules. The fourth front-end module handles payment. Available options range from payment with credit card using SSL (secure socket layer, a low level protocol) or using SET (secure electronic transaction, a high level protocol for credit card payment), to true digital money e-Cash), where the money to pay for the goods is actually stored on the hard disk of the user.

The middle tier resides on the servers of the merchant or its Internet access provider. A Web application server takes care of transaction properties, security, access control, and also ensures adequate performance. Additional modules can provide more sophisticated filtering and user profiling

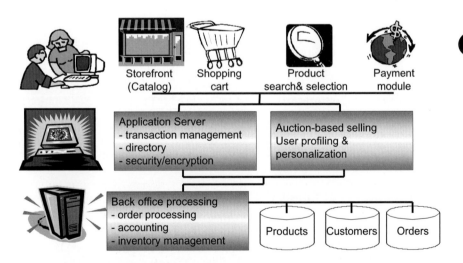

Fig. 4.20 Integrated e-commerce shopping mall architecture.

Fig. 4.21   Virtual Mall @ ActiveWorlds.

mechanisms, to present customized offerings to users based on their preferences and previous buying behaviour. Novel ways of pricing goods such as auction-based selling can also be included.

The lowest tier contains the databases: The products database, the customer database, and the orders database. Order fulfilment happens on this level. Depending on the degree of integration, orders can simply be printed out, and then be processed manually. If the company has already integrated its business processes, it might want to link its enterprise resource planning system with the shopping mall. EPR vendors like SAP, but also e-business vendors like IBM are already selling integrated packages linking the electronic storefront with accounting and controlling, production and materials management, quality management and plant maintenance, sales and distribution.

As long as all the systems working together are from the same vendor, integration is straightforward (at least in the vendor product documentation). Unfortunately, a supply chain usually links systems from many vendors. RosettaNet is trying to define a standard of how various products can communicate with each other in the supply chain.

4.7.6 RosettaNet – defining the IT supply chain

RosettaNet (www.rosettanet.org) is a consortium of large industry firms and software vendors which defines electronic business interfaces for the IT supply chain. The goal is to define, for example, how a part number is displayed or how inventory queries can be made through a standard interface. This should result in a unified form of product information and a common taxonomy.

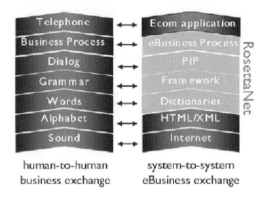

Fig. 4.22 Motivation for RosettaNet (source: RosettaNet).

Resellers should get standardized ordering/return procedures and system interfaces to distributors. End-users should get effective procurement through uniform templates, which can be contextually linked to government authorized schedules.

RosettaNet motivates the need for such common electronic business interfaces in the following diagram, displaying the parallel between a human-to-human business exchange and a server-to-server electronic business exchange: In order to communicate in a human-to-human business exchange, humans must be able to produce and hear sound. Further, they must then agree on a common alphabet, used to create individual words. Grammatical rules are then applied to the words to create a dialogue. That dialogue forms the business process, which is conducted, for example, by phone.

RosettaNet compares the fundamental system of exchanging sounds in a human-to-human business exchange to the Internet, which enables two servers to exchange information during a server-to-server electronic business exchange. HTML/XML functions as the "alphabet" of this electronic exchange. e-Commerce applications serve as the instrument by which an electronic business process is transmitted.

The missing elements in order to scale e-business are the dictionaries, the framework, the Partner Interface Processes (PIPs) and the e-business processes. RosettaNet fills this existing gap by focusing on building a master dictionary to define properties for products, partners, and business transactions. This master dictionary, coupled with exchange protocols, is used to support the e-business dialogue known as the Partner Interface Process or PIP. RosettaNet PIPs create new areas of alignment within the overall IT supply-chain e-business processes, allowing IT supply-chain partners to scale e-business, and to fully leverage e-commerce applications and the Internet as a business-to-business commerce tool.

Figure 4.23 describes the process used to create RosettaNet's common PIPs.

Business process modelling is used to identify and quantify the individual elements of a business process, creating a clearly defined model of the supply chain partner interfaces as they exist today. This is called "as is" modelling. Through the analysis of the detailed "as is" model (the "business process analysis"), a "generic to-be" process emerges, showing the opportunities for

Fig. 4.23 Business process modelling for partner interface processes (PIPs) (source: RosettaNet).

re-alignment in the form of a PIP target list, and estimating the business impact of implementing the resulting PIPs (savings as a function of time and money). The purpose of each PIP is to provide common business data models and documents, enabling system developers to implement the RosettaNet e-business interfaces. Each PIP includes:

- XML documents based on implementation framework DTDs, specifying PIP services, transactions, and messages.
- Class and sequence diagrams in UML (unified modelling language).*
- Validation tool.
- Implementation guide.

As part of RosettaNet's foundational projects, two data dictionaries have been developed to provide a common set of properties required by PIPs. The first is a technical properties dictionary containing technical specifications for all product categories, and the second is a business properties dictionary which includes catalogue properties, partner properties (attributes used to describe supply chain partner companies) and business transaction properties. These dictionaries, coupled with the RosettaNet implementation framework (exchange protocol), form the basis for each RosettaNet PIP. RosettaNet also encompasses the Electronic Components (EC) supply chain.

Besides RosettaNet there is also Collaborative Planning Forecasting and Replenishment (CPFR), a business model that proposes a holistic approach to supply chain management. CPFR starts by setting up an agreement between two trading partners. A forecast can then be frozen in advance to be converted into shipping plans with the goal of avoiding customary order processing.

While RosettaNet and CPFR try to support supply chain integration by standardization, Microsoft tries to do the same by its market dominance. SAP, Ariba, and I2 attempt to define proprietary standards by becoming the dominant player in the market, an approach that Microsoft has pioneered with sweeping success in the operating system area, and it now trying to leverage into the e-business domain.

---

*UML is a standard defined by CASE (Computer Aided Software Engineering) tool vendors. It is used to specify the behavior of complex systems in an open way.

4.7.7 Microsoft's BizTalk framework initiative (www.biztalk.org)

Microsoft has defined its own XML-based EDI framework for e-commerce: *BizTalk* is a design framework for implementing an XML schema and set of XML tags used in messages sent between applications. By defining a technical vocabulary for describing common business processes in e-commerce and across specific industries, BizTalk gives companies the opportunity to link up with customers and partners in meaningful ways over the Internet. BizTalk defines business schemas for corporate purchasing, product catalogues, offers, promotional campaigns and other business processes. BizTalk also should make integrating software easier: because BizTalk is a cross-platform framework, it allows software to communicate between different common object models, programming languages or shared database schemas.

The BizTalk Framework includes a design framework for implementing an XML schema and a set of XML tags used in messages sent between applications. BizTalk Framework schemas – business documents and messages expressed in XML – will be registered and stored on www.BizTalk.org. Anybody can download the framework and use it to implement XML schemas. As long as the schemas pass a verification test, they are valid BizTalk Framework schemas. The www.BizTalk.org Web site provides an automated submission and validation process. Businesses also have the option of publishing their schemas on the BizTalk Web site in a secure area for private use between trading partners.

By formalizing the process of expressing business process interchanges in a consistent and extensible format, the BizTalk Framework makes it easier for software developers to map from one business process to another, enabling faster adoption of electronic interchange in a wide variety of industries using XML. The BizTalk Framework provides a platform for migrating an existing set of industry interchange standards to XML, specifically targeted towards the EDI community.

The BizTalk Framework assumes that application programs are distinct entities, and application integration takes place using a loosely coupled message-passing approach. For two applications to exchange XML messages using the BizTalk Framework, the two applications simply need to be able to format, transmit, receive, and consume a standardized XML message. Microsoft is developing a BizTalk Server that automates many of the functions required in a BizTalk Framework interchange. For example, the webMethods B2B server is also capable of supporting the BizTalk Framework interchange.

Dozens of industry organizations and standards bodies are actively engaged in the definition of XML schemas for application integration. These groups include e-commerce consortia like RosettaNet and Commerce.Net, software industry groups like the Open Applications Group (OAG) and the Object Management Group (OMG), vertical industry standards bodies like Acord (insurance) and HL7 (healthcare), and individual software companies like Ariba and Commerce One. Each one of these efforts has the goal of defining a standard set of XML documents used in an interchange between applications or between companies. Ariba, Commerce One, and OAG have already signed on to the BizTalk initiative as charter members of the steering committee.

4

4.7.8 Hewlett-Packard's e-services and e-speak

Besides Microsoft, HP is also trying to push its own e-business vision, based on e-services and e-speak. HP is suggesting a fully automated, agent-based approach. HP envisions that computer agents will be moving around on networks freely, communicating and closing deals on behalf of their human owners. To reach that goal, HP suggests e-speak as the underlying communications language and e-services as the communication metaphor.

To motivate the need for e-services, HP makes the following argument: initially, there were isolated Web sites, which prospective buyers had to visit sequentially one after the other, to manually locate the goods and services they were looking for (Fig. 4.24). Then, sites were combined into portals, where all services around a common topic were offered. Initially, customers of a travel portal had to manually put together their itinerary, combining plane schedules and fares, car rentals, and hotel reservations. Today, we are beginning to see integrated offerings, applying business logic to make the task for the user as simple as possible. For a travel Web site, this means that travellers have to enter their schedule and preferences only once. Then the Web site automatically chooses plane flights, car rentals, and hotel reservations based on their wishes. This integrated vision is what HP calls e-services.

In order for e-services to succeed, three prerequisites need to be fulfilled:

- First, the wiring needs to be available. Employees, clients, and business partners of everybody wanting to participate in e-services have to be connected to the Internet.

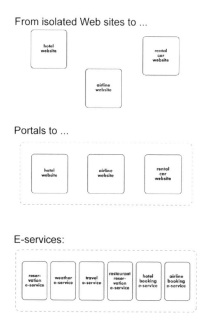

Fig. 4.24 From Web sites to portals to e-services (Source: Hewlett-Packard).

- Second, the key business processes that should become e-services enabled need to get integrated between companies.
- Third, a critical mass of consumers needs to be on-line; otherwise there will not be enough end users of the system.

e-Services should make Web-based business processes much easier to implement. e-Services are modular services and IT resources available on the Net – they describe what they are capable of doing, they talk to each other, and they can band together to complete a given task. For example, in an e-services world, an e-services portal lets you book your trip. And because all the e-services communicate with each other, when your flight is delayed, everything else is adjusted – automatically. Or in a diabetes affinity group, information about new cures, new drug discussions, cooking recipes, and hosted chat sessions can all be linked.

e-Speak is the core technology to enable e-services. It is very similar to Microsoft's BizTalk, also defining a language for business processes to talk to each other. e-Services are supposed to communicate using e-speak regardless of the technology platform they were built on. Once powered by e-speak, e-services can advertise their capabilities to other e-services, discover other e-services on the Net, and even align with other e-services on the fly to create new e-services. In essence, e-speak makes every e-speak-enabled e-service a potential building block for creating other e-services. HP hopes that entire ecosystems of e-services will grow and change dynamically as new e-services advertise their capabilities over the Net.

e-Speak makes possible the concept of "dynamic brokering": e-speak technology can insert an electronic mediator to bid, broker, and build the right set of resources or services to complete a particular request (Fig. 4.25).

Users will not have to go to a web site anymore, if they do not want to. They will be able to make a request, and a broker will search for the best service on their behalf – based on parameters they specify, such as price, time, convenience, quality, reliability, safety record, etc. This capability will turn

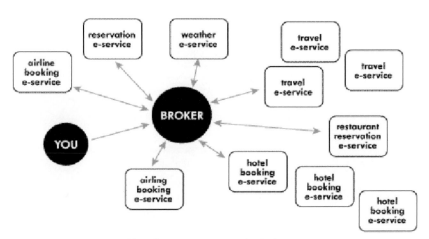

Fig. 4.25 Dynamic e-services brokering.

the Web into an open-services marketplace where e-services are composed specifically to work on behalf of the user.

HP has had a hard time in the e-business area. So far, attention has focused on other IT vendors like Sun, IBM, or Microsoft. By advertising the e-services concept heavily, HP hopes to establish itself again as an e-business leader; and e-services and e-speak as the de facto standard for business-to-business e-commerce.

4.7.9 The UN ETO system

The United Nation's ETO (Electronic Trading Opportunity) system has become a de facto standard for third-world SMEs (small- and medium-sized enterprises) participating in world trade almost without advertisement (Fig. 4.26). The ETO system has been developed by Unctad, the United Nations Conference on Trade and Development. It is based on the Internet newsreader Netnews. It is a bulletin board for posting "for sale" and "wanted" ads to a global audience. Everything from soy beans to oil tankers can be put up there by anybody on the globe. The ETO newsgroup is one of the largest Internet newsgroups.

ETO is the most widely used service of the UN Trade Point program (see Section 1.1). The ETO system has become one of the predominate sources of international trade leads and is utilized by businesses world-wide (not exclusively by Trade Points). It is key as a source of trade leads primarily for developing countries. Many governments redistribute ETOs through their own on-line

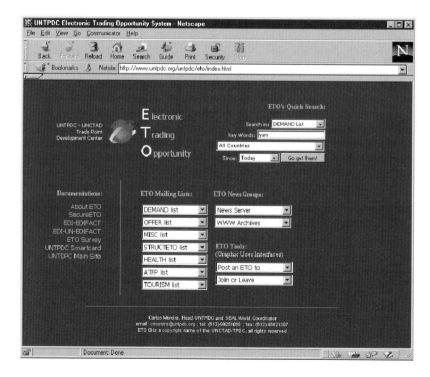

Fig. 4.26 The UN ETO (Electronic Trading Opportunity) system.

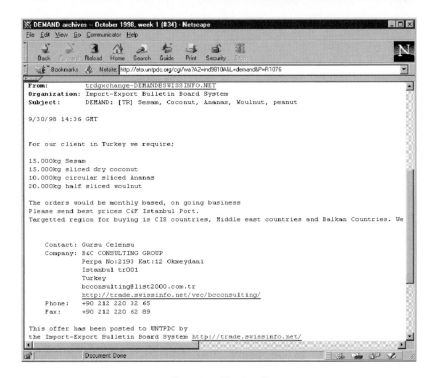

Fig. 4.26   (Continued)

information services. However, the usefulness of the ETO system is being degraded by the large amount of advertising that is being done by various export companies, particularly in Asia.

Currently many Trade Points are doing some manual fixing of ETOs on their own. In an improved ETO system the sender of a message should be authorized and uniquely identified and ETO messages should be filtered to only deliver relevant messages to each client – not for sending marketing information.

SETO (Secure ETO) (Fig. 4.27) is the extension of the ETO system to electronically support the whole trading process, from matchmaking, over

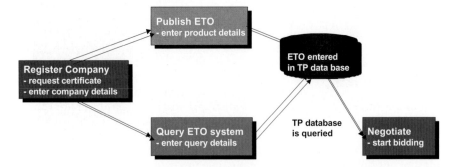

Fig. 4.27   The Secure ETO system covering the whole trading process.

negotiation, to payment and shipment arrangement. A prototype with public domain components has been built by the UN, a reference implementation based on commercial products is available.

The SETO system, which requires registration of the organization issuing ETOs with Trade Points offers a much higher level of quality of trade opportunities. SETO should operate as an extension and in parallel with the current ETO system.

The ETO and SETO systems clearly illustrate one of the main problems of information systems: Finding the information one is looking for. The trader using the ETO system is inundated with useless advertisements, and needs to spend valuable time every day to scan through the message flood to filter out the few messages that are of use to him.

4.8 Critical technology success factors for e-business transformation

This chapter has discussed a broad range of technologies that make the e-business transformation possible. First of all, to make the transformation work, a company needs to have a sound strategy and business model, anchored in the core business area of the company, be it manufacturing, services, or a totally new industry domain. But from the very beginning, while developing the strategy and business model, the company needs to keep in mind the capabilities of e-business technology. These technological capabilities are the enablers of totally new application areas and industries. To successfully e-business enable a company, there are some critical success factors that are absolutely crucial.

First of all, to implement e-business means to successfully complete an *IT systems integration* project with all the bells and whistles. In particular, legacy systems that still are the backbone of a company's IT infrastructure need to be successfully integrated with the latest generation object-oriented three-tier systems. Interface standards like CORBA, DCOM, or IIOP, and *middleware* products like MQ/Series, Tuxedo, and Orbix need to be evaluated to find the best way to reliably integrate heterogeneous systems.

The *security issues* that plagued the Internet in the first few years of its existence have been mostly *solved*. Firewalls, digital certificates, and encryption allow companies to make their networks and Web sites almost as secure as the phone system. And as with the phone system, security is never 100% watertight – there are always tiny loopholes where villains can sneak in. However the overwhelming majority of those loopholes are not there through deficiencies in technology, but by the user. Disgruntled employees that erase the hard disks of the corporate computers or negligent users forgetting their passwords are by far the largest security risks. Digital payment systems, on the other hand, are still in the fermenting stage. Internet users can now safely pay by credit card – SSL and SET have become de facto standards, but the market for bill payment and presentment is still crowded by many, incompatible systems, none of which has already obtained a critical mass. Very soon we will be able to pay most of our bills on-line, but it is impossible to say today which one will be the winning payment system.

Over the first 2 years of its existence *XML* has quickly become the *lingua franca of the Internet*. It is not only a better, more flexible HTML, but it is used to integrate all sorts of processes and applications. For the first time, companies have a common vocabulary for exchanging data and manipulating this data concurrently. The full syntax and semantic of the new language is still emerging, there are many different dialects such as BizTalk, cXML, RosettaNet, and e-speak, to name just a few. We can expect that it will still be some time before the dominant dialect for each application domain emerges. But XML is here today, and it is here to stay! It already helps greatly today in integrating heterogeneous processes spanning many previously incompatible systems.

There is no longer a need to keep "reinventing the wheel" by implementing business processes with custom-built software. In areas ranging from sales force automation, procurement, call centres, manufacturing, supply chain management, to accounting, there are *e-business enabled standard packages* fully supporting all aspects of the business process. Vendors like Siebel, Ariba, SAP, I2, etc. are offering software packages that fully integrate with legacy systems and the Internet. While deployment of any of these packages is primarily a systems integration task, the role of the company is to fully understand the business processes to be automated. The company's IT staff and third party consultants can then customize the packages to support the company's process automation. Seamless integration of business processes over company boundaries is possible using open Internet standards. XML has taken on the role of the proprietary systems for EDI, enabling the integration of workflows over the Internet.

The main asset of a company, its *knowledge,* needs to be nurtured appropriately. IT can greatly support this task. Document management systems, groupware, and company-wide Intranets provide an excellent infrastructure for managing knowledge. But the goal should be much more ambitious, to foster a culture of knowledge sharing, making information accessible to everyone who needs it. It should be one of the primary concerns of any company to support optimal collaboration among its employees. While groupware systems like Lotus Notes or Microsoft Exchange support this task, there are now simpler-to-use Web-based out-of-the-box systems that support virtual teams that are working all around the globe, continuously creating new knowledge for the benefit of the company.

4

5 Tools for managing knowledge

Introduction	Definitions of: ▶ e-Commerce ▶ e-Business ▶ Knowledge management
1 Dispelling the myths of e-business	▶ Income gaps between industrialized countries and 3rd World ▶ Re-distribution of wealth in society ▶ Isolation of individual
2 Turning business into e-business	▶ e-Business transformation ▶ Business process outsourcing ▶ Portals ▶ Case study: pharmaceutical industry ▶ Case study: dating over the Web
3 Blueprint for e-business implementation	▶ The information process integration blueprint ▶ e-Business deployment roadmap ▶ Knowledge management deployment ▶ e-Business project management
4 Key e-business technologies	▶ XML overview ▶ Security and digital money ▶ Virtual collaboration ▶ Workflow management ▶ Process integration by packageware
5 Tools for managing knowledge	▶ MIT process handbook ▶ Knowledge navigation

5

Knowledge about its business processes is one of the core assets of a company. The MIT Process Handbook provides a vehicle for managing this knowledge. In the crucial area of domain knowledge acquisition, gathering, storage, retrieval and navigation, complete packages are not yet available to cover the whole process.

This chapter discusses the following topics.
- Managing process knowledge: the MIT Process Handbook
- Managing domain knowledge: Knowledge navigation

The major challenges for a company in this new century are to stop the knowledge drain and to convert loss of knowledge into knowledge acquisition. In order to achieve these ambitious goals, implicit as well as explicit knowledge needs to be treated as the company's core asset.

Implicit knowledge gathering and acquisition starts and continues inside people's heads. While IT can at best provide auxiliary support to implicit knowledge acquisition and storage, it is crucial for all aspects of the management of explicit knowledge, starting from acquiring and formalizing, to storing and retrieving knowledge.

A fundamental part of explicit business knowledge is knowledge about business processes. There is just one tool that I am aware of whose goal it is to store all the business processes of the major corporations – this tool is the MIT Process Handbook. It provides a well-thought-out repository and a methodology for the capture, storage, and retrieval of business processes.

How to manage and make accessible the other form of knowledge, domain knowledge, is discussed in the second section of this chapter

5.1 The MIT Process Handbook

Most multinational companies as well as many mid-sized firms have gone through the iterations of business process reengineering. As a prerequisite for successful process reengineering, companies need to get a grasp on their own processes. Many company-wide process mapping projects have been started, where the goal was to create an organization-wide process map, a repository of all core business processes in the company. These projects have built huge repositories of processes, but little practical success has resulted from all this work. The reasons for failure are manifold. Processes change too quickly for the process maps to be updated in a timely fashion, perhaps because of mergers and acquisitions, internal reorganizations, or because new products are brought to market in a quick succession. Another frequent reason for failure is that the main project sponsor leaves before the process-mapping project is completed. Finally, it can turn out that the systems and methodologies used were inappropriate.

Based on possible reasons for failure in firm-wide process-mapping projects, we can define the following requirements for a process mapping and repository method and tool:

- It needs to adapt to rapidly changing environments and processes. Company strategies are now adjusted at least once every year, new products are brought to market every month, and companies are reorganized, merged, or acquired at a still increasing pace. This means that processes can be different for every product, they might change at a day's notice, and new processes as well as variants of old processes might be added every day.
- It needs to handle increasing complexity well. A few processes with dozens of process steps are easily handled by a flowcharting system. But a large corporation has hundreds of business processes, which have hundreds of process steps, involving many participants around the globe. These processes need to be described in an easily understandable way, but still require a powerful process database management system capable of handling thousands of processes, where each process can occur in many different variants.
- The process repository and a process-oriented way of thinking need to be made a part of the corporate culture. The whole process-mapping project is worthless if it is not put to use. Not only the CEO and its corporate strategy planning staff, but also line managers and process owners need to perceive the process map as a crucial resource for the creation of new business, for business improvement and process redesign.

Tom Malone and his group at the Center for Coordination Science at MIT's Sloan School of Business have been working on such a system for the past 7 years. The Process Handbook is a tool for sharing and managing business knowledge and for helping to redesign and improve business processes.

"It is intended to help people: (1) redesign existing organizational processes, (2) invent new organizational processes (especially ones that take advantage of information technology), (3) learn about organizations, and (4) automatically generate software to support organizational processes" (Malone et al., 1997).

The Process Handbook project pursues two main goals:

(1) Developing methodologies and software tools for representing and codifying business processes at varying levels of abstraction. These methodologies are based on the software engineering concept of inheritance and on coordination theory about managing dependencies, pioneered by Tom Malone and his group.
(2) Collecting, organizing, and analyzing numerous example processes of how different groups or companies perform similar functions. Currently there are about 5000 core processes from diverse business areas stored in the process repository.

The on-line version of the Process Handbook provides a resource which people interested in improving organizational processes can consult to find a variety of alternative ways for performing particular processes, along with experiences and guidelines about which alternatives work best in differing situations. One of the main advantages of the Process Handbook is that it allows people to explicitly represent similarities and differences among related processes. This allows somebody doing process reengineering to easily find alternatives for how a given process could be performed.

5.1.1 Uses of the Process Handbook

The developers of the Process Handbook envision four main uses for their methodology and software tools:

(1) Imagine new organizations and processes. The Process Handbook should be an enabler for the invention of new organizational forms and processes. The process representation technique and the software tools make it possible to suggest new organizational processes based on existing ones. As the biggest change in the business world is the increasing use of IT, the Process Handbook can be used to explore new business processes that will be enabled by pervasive IT.

(2) Redesigning existing organizations. Nearly all large organizations today are engaged in some kind of systematic effort to redesign their business processes. The Process Handbook is ideally suited to create an "as-is" company-wide process repository that can be used as a basis for the reengineered "to-be" processes.

(3) Sharing "best practice" business processes. Because the handbook contains a database of processes and a methodology for comparing those processes, it can also provide a particularly valuable resource for collecting and analyzing so-called best practices. The 5000+ processes stored today in the Process Handbook provide a useful source of ideas and examples for people with differing backgrounds, ranging from consultants doing process reengineering to employees moving to a new job where they want to learn how things are done. Particular emphasis is put on collecting e-business relevant best practice processes.

(4) Generating software to support the processes. For instance, previously developed workflow software (e.g. templates) can be organized according to the process descriptions contained in the Process Handbook. More interestingly, the processes represented in the handbook could be used to help automatically drive the creation of new software customized to specific situations.

For example, when managers in a company want to install a new workflow management system to support the hiring process, they might first consult the Process Handbook to see a variety of alternative hiring processes used in different organizations. They might, for instance, see examples of different approaches to advertising, interviewing, salary determination, and making offers. After comparing various choices, they can combine elements of different alternatives and modify the resulting process to fit their needs. When they have selected a process they want, they can ask the system to generate a workflow system customized to their process, using libraries of previously developed workflow scripts. Packages with human resources software modules such as SAP, Baan, Oracle, or Peoplesoft support this approach.

5.1.2 Specializations of business processes

Similarly to most process representation techniques, the Process Handbook uses the notion of decomposition: a process can be broken down or "decomposed" into subparts (also called "subactivities"). In addition to this concept of decomposition, the Process Handbook also includes the concept of *specialization*: a process can be differentiated or "specialized" into various specializations. Thus, while a subactivity represents a part of a process, a specialization represents a "way of" doing the process. Using this concept, processes can be arranged in a hierarchical network with very generic processes at the top and increasingly specialized processes at lower levels. As in object-oriented programming, the specialized processes can automatically inherit properties of their more generic "parents", except where they explicitly add or change a property.

Figure 5.1 illustrates how decomposition and specialization can work together to model a business process hierarchy: The generic activity called "Sell product" is decomposed into subactivities like "Identify potential customers" and "Inform potential customers". The generic activity is also specialized into more focused activities like "Sell by mail order" and "Sell in retail store". These specialized activities automatically inherit the subactivities and other characteristics of their parent process. If needed, the specialized processes can change the decompositions they inherit. For instance, in "Sell by mail order", the subactivities of "delivering a product" and "receiving payment" are inherited without modification, but "Identify potential customers" is replaced by the more specialized activity of "Obtaining mailing lists".

Sibling specialization processes can be collected into bundles. Figure 5.2 shows part of the specialization hierarchy for sales processes. Items in brackets (such as "[Sell how?]") are bundles that group together sets of related specializations. Items in bold have further specializations. In this example, one bundle of specializations for "Sell something" is related to how the sale is made: direct mail, retail store, or direct sales. Another bundle of specializations has to do with what is being sold: beer, automotive components, financial services, etc.

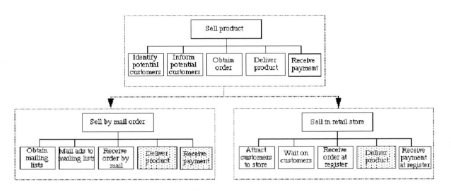

Fig. 5.1 Sample representations of a hierarchy of three different sales processes
(source: Malone *et al.*, 1999).

5

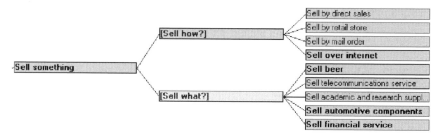

Fig. 5.2 Summary display showing bundles of specializations of the activity "Sell something" (Source: Malone *et al.*, 1999).

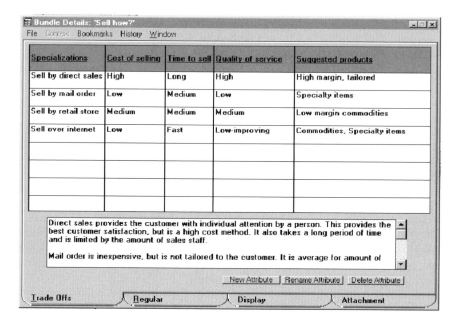

Fig. 5.3 A tradeoff table showing typical advantages and disadvantages of different specializations for the generic sales process (source: Malone *et al.*, 1999).

These bundles can then be used to compare the relative merits of the alternative sibling processes using a tradeoff table. For example, Fig. 5.3 shows a tradeoff table that compares alternatives in terms of their ratings on various criteria; different specializations are the rows and different characteristics are the columns. Comparisons in the cells of the table may be the result of systematic studies, but in some cases they may be simply rough guesses by knowledgeable managers or consultants.

5.1.3 The Process Handbook software tools

The Process Handbook software consists of a series of tools for storing and manipulating process descriptions. The tools allow people to explicitly represent the similarities (and differences) among related processes to easily find sensible alternatives for how a given process could be performed. The core system manages the database of process descriptions and displays and edits selected entries. The current system runs on Windows PCs and is implemented in Visual Basic and several productivity tools such as the Visio drawing tool. The process descriptions are stored in a relational database (currently Microsoft Access). The PC system allows users to retrieve, view and edit process descriptions as well as adding new specializations. The screen shots of Figs 5.1–5.3 have been produced using the PC version. There is also a Web interface allowing users of standard Web browsers to view (but not change) the contents of the Process Handbook from anywhere on the Internet.

Figure 5.4 displays the specialization view of the process "Sell over the Internet". The Process Compass in the upper left corner shows two dimensions for analyzing business processes. The vertical dimension distinguishes different parts of a process; the horizontal dimension distinguishes different types of processes. It allows a user to drill down into a specialization or to go up in the inheritance hierarchy to a generalization (types of processes). It also allows decomposing an activity into subactivities or navigating upwards to see how a subactivity is part of a broader activity (parts of processes).

The activity "Sell over Internet" is part of the bundle "Sell electronically", and consists of specialization bundles "Sell over Internet how" and "Sell over Internet views".

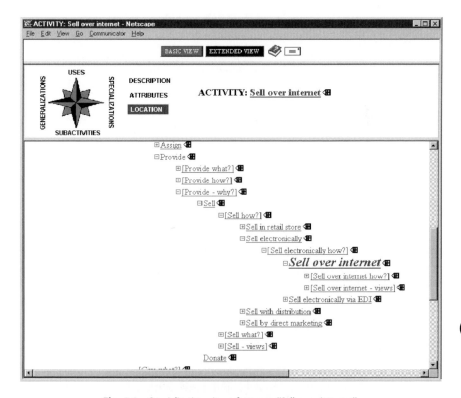

Fig. 5.4 Specialization view of process "Sell over Internet".

Fig. 5.5   Decomposition view of process "Sell over Internet".

Figure 5.5 depicts the "Sell over Internet" process decomposed into its subactivities. Subactivities in the shaded cells are different from their parent generalizations.

Besides the Process Handbook software tools, there are numerous other process tools available, such as flowcharting tools, simulation tools, workflow systems, and Computer-Aided Software Engineering (CASE) tools. To be able to move processes back and forth between these different tools, the Process Handbook team organized a working group that has developed a Process Interchange Format (PIF) for moving process descriptions between systems that use diverse representations. Via PIF, a process in one system (e.g. a process modeller) can be used by another (say, a simulator), whose result in turn can be used by yet another system. Each system uses as much as possible of the process descriptions and passes on information it cannot understand to other systems.

The Process Handbook team has recently started a company, Phios (www.phios.com). Phios markets the three components of the Process Handbook, namely the process repository server, giving Web access to the relational Process Handbook database; the process editor for the creation and maintenance of the process knowledge stored in the repository; and the business process knowledge including the more than 5000 processes, case examples, and best practices collected for the Process Handbook.

The Process Handbook puts an excellent process knowledge acquisition and management tool for e-business transformation into the hands of business managers. They can collect the existing business processes to assess their readiness for e-business using the Process Handbook process repository and editor tools. They can then compare and benchmark the existing processes with best-practice processes in the Process Handbook to come up with innovative new ideas for the implementation of the reengineered e-business enabled processes. As a side benefit they have the specification of the new and reengineered processes in the Process Handbook to be used for documentation, for continuous reengineering, and for the training of employees.

While the Process Handbook has unique characteristics for process knowledge acquisition and management, the situation is less clear for gathering and managing domain knowledge. There are numerous methods and tools available, but no clear leader has emerged. The next section describes methods, techniques, and tools for gathering, visualizing, retrieving and filtering domain knowledge.

5.2 Knowledge navigation

We have never had as much information at our fingertips as we do today, but we have never been more helpless in using it. Everybody speaks about knowledge management, but companies have never been less competent at retaining knowledge while having to cope with an increasingly mobile workforce. Successful companies so far have worked rather by providing a successful culture of knowledge sharing than by using the latest IT knowledge management gadgets to their full. As discussed at the beginning of the chapter, knowledge management is a process which starts inside people's heads and is mainly based on changing the mindset by creating a culture of knowledge sharing, although "techknowledgy" is clearly a part of knowledge management (Davenport and Prusak, 1997, p. 123). As Davenport notes, the "availability of certain new technologies such as Lotus Notes and the World Wide Web has been instrumental in catalyzing the knowledge management movement".

This section looks at the tools and technologies for managing domain knowledge. On the technology level, this is essentially how to store and find information in corporate Intranets.

To make knowledge accessible, there are three dimensions to be dealt with (Fig. 5.6): Most important is *information content*. Quality of the information is absolutely crucial to the usefulness of the knowledge base. Stale, imprecise, or incomplete information cannot be compensated for by perfect packaging. What is in the system is far more valuable than all the bells and whistles of the

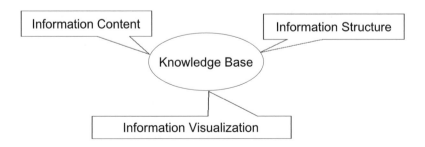

Fig. 5.6 Dimensions of organizing knowledge.

GUI and search technology; fancy search features are worthless if the system does not contain valuable date. On the other hand the best data is without value if it is not accessible or is hidden underneath an unusable GUI. This means that also the second dimension, *information visualization*, is absolutely crucial. As each marketing expert knows, customers buy with their eyes, which means that information needs to be optimally visualized. The best information is useless if it cannot be found. Gems of information content are of little or no use if access to it is only possible by following 14 hierarchical submenus. This means that the third dimension, *structuring information* is equally important. Structuring information means making information ready in such a way that it can be accessed quickly and efficiently.

5.2.1 Structured, semi-structured, and unstructured information

Information in corporate Intranets is available in abundant quantities, although normally not in a form that ensures consistently high quality. This information comes in many formats: legacy systems and ERP systems such as SAP or PeopleSoft provide structured information in relational databases, collaborative systems such as Lotus Notes or Microsoft Exchange contain semi-structured information, while the corporate Intranet Web contains unstructured information. Making these various information sources accessible in a unified interface provides a daunting challenge. But structuring information also means the need to make a conscious decision on whether information is best collected and accessed in structured, semi-structured, or unstructured format.

In structured information each field has a closely defined meaning. In Fig. 5.7, for the field "Smoking" there are only four possible values: "prefer not to say", "don't smoke", "smoke occasionally", "smoke regularly". Structured information is usually stored in relational databases and can be encoded efficiently. Searching is straightforward in structured information. It is, for example, very simple to search for all people that don't smoke. The problem is

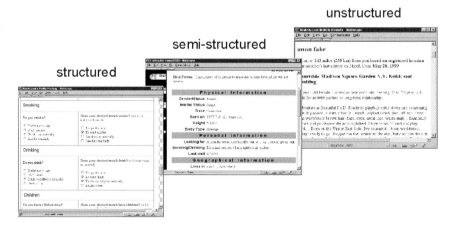

Fig. 5.7   From structured to semi-structured to unstructured information.

to enter "unplanned for" information into a structured database. There is no way in our example for somebody to say that he smokes the pipe, something which might make a difference if somebody is looking for a partner to live with.

Unstructured information is normally in full-text format. This makes it easy to enter any type of information, but it also makes it hard to locate information. For example, in a classified ad I can say what I want in the language I like, and can describe myself in as colourful words as I want, "as a playful PhD looking to settle down in passion". This might attract the right type of companion, if she finds my profile by browsing the whole database. But, I might forget to mention my smoking habits, because the database does not force me to fill in that field. Also, there is no simple way in an unstructured database to find "all people that don't smoke".

Semi-structured information is somewhere in the middle. There are fields that need to be filled in, as in structured information, but the fields can be completed in the way that the user wants. An example is again provided in Fig. 5.7. Here the woman in Zurich is given a chance to find her "Ideal Person", "... someone to make me scream beyond my wildest dreams". In her personal profile, she has to define that she is a "light smoker". This allows, after some tweaking in the search form, a search for all non-smoking people. Lotus Notes typically contains semi-structured information. For searching, semi-structured information is extremely useful, because knowledge about the field structure can be used to narrow down a search. On the other hand, the semi-structured information format allows one the relative freedom of not only establishing that he smokes, but also to say that he is a pipe smoker.

There is an even more structured way to represent knowledge, which has been pioneered in the field of artificial intelligence (AI). What if computers could reason and draw conclusions on their own. In order to do so, they need to have common-sense knowledge, stored in a format they can understand. The CYC project started over 10 years ago to build up a machine-readable database of common-sense knowledge.

5.2.2 CYC: Describing common-sense knowledge

The CYC project is a large-scale project that was initiated by MCC (Microelectronics and Computer Technology Corporation in Austin, Texas, a joint research consortium sponsored by the US industry). It has been led from the beginning by its visionary leader, Doug Lenat and has recently been spun off into a commercial company, CYC (www.cyc.com). The goal of CYC is to build a very large knowledge base containing a broad range of common-sense knowledge. The CYC knowledge base consists of a network of units or frames, where each unit corresponds to a physical object or an abstract concept. The knowledge base incorporates millions of everyday terms, concepts, facts, and rules of thumb that comprise human consensus reality – that is, common sense. The CYC interface has the ability to communicate in a natural language, such as English. That ability is used to further enlarge the knowledge base.

The CYC system includes an immense multi-contextual knowledge base, an inference engine, a set of interface tools, and a number of special-purpose application modules.

5

To promote CYC's use, Doug Lenat has defined 10 exemplary CYC applications:

(1) Advice services: Offer a service over a network that helps people select which type of new car to buy.

(2) Directed marketing: Use a person's buying history to infer their hobbies, interests, occupation, physical needs and preferences, etc. From that model, decide which products to try to sell them, and what argument to use to convince them they should buy the product.

(3) On-line brokering of goods or services: Using a common vocabulary and shared fundamental knowledge about transactions, enable a large set of buyers and sellers to find each other and to negotiate deals – on-line and (semi-)automatically.

(4) Database cleaning: Relate a database's fields and keys to CYC predicates and terms, and use CYC's common-sense constraints to detect possible errors and inconsistencies in that database.

(5) Database integration: Use that same sort of "articulation" approach to have several heterogeneous databases all relate their contents to one central knowledge base. Use this to (1) detect and resolve contradictions among databases, and (2) handle queries that require accessing – and integrating the results from – multiple databases.

(6) Corporate knowledge assets management: Represent a company's know-how, policies, important documents, programs, and databases – all in a form that a program can effectively reason with. Use this as an on-line policy manual or as a sort of "smart Yellow Pages" for employees.

(7) Smart spreadsheets: Explain the meaning of the rows and columns by tying them to a large corpus of general knowledge about occupations, human capabilities, goals, household objects, etc. Highlight abnormal (though not illegal) values and suggest places where there seems to be a missing equation or constraint.

(8) Smarter interfaces: Use an on-line model of the meaning of what the application program is doing, what the user's goals are, what constraints they are under (e.g. deadlines), etc. to adjust the interface. For example reorder questions on a form; rearrange windows; highlight or cross-out various parts; guess at values to fill in certain blanks; and so on.

(9) Machine translation of technical documents: Provide a set of flexible templates into which 95% of some class of technical documents (e.g. installation instructions for a laser printer) can be captured. Then, using currently available natural language software, process such documents, converting them into a set of filled template instances. Conversely, the "first writing" of a manual could itself be done by filling out such templates. Translations into different languages could then be produced by composing the translations of each template. Difficult portions get flagged for checking by hand.

(10) Enriched artificial reality: Create simulated "worlds" in which physical objects behave "realistically" and machine-run people behave "intelligently" – particularly when one interacts with those objects and persons in ways that were not specifically preconceived.

CYC stores its information in a highly specialized format, which is only understandable to experts and the CYC system itself. Of the information stored in a company's Intranet, 99% is in full-text format. Systems like CYC can be used to make better use of this vast quantity of information by enabling applications like the ones listed above. Besides CYC, there are a rapidly growing number of tools, techniques, and methods for making knowledge accessible. The next section gives a survey of these tools.

5.2.3 Making knowledge accessible – four design concepts for navigation

The orientation and information exploration problem can easily be experienced by anybody browsing on the Web: How often in a browsing session did the reader inadvertently stumble on an interesting site, only to search desperately for the same site in the next session? Also called the problem of *being lost in hyperspace,* this issue has met high attention in the hypertext and knowledge management research community, and many different solutions have been proposed.

In our Web design work we have identified four main concepts that need to be considered when designing the knowledge structure of a document: *linking, searching, mapping*, and *agents*. Applying these concepts when designing a knowledge management system make the information much more accessible. This section illustrates the four concepts by a large collection of practical examples, simultaneously using the four design concepts to classify existing tools for knowledge navigation and management.

Figure 5.8 illustrates the four concepts and their underlying principles.

The *linking* structure is the most distinguishing feature of a hypertext document such as an HTML Web page. Links allow direct access to a designated location within the information space through markers that are embedded into the documents. Simply clicking with the mouse on a hot spot on the screen brings the reader to the linked destination. For novice or first-time users it can be very helpful to reduce the complexity of the linked

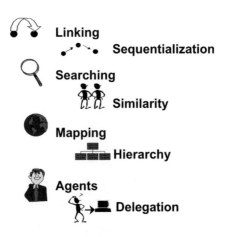

Fig. 5.8   Design for navigation.

hypertext document to one dimension by offering them a *sequential* path or guided tour through the hyperdocument.

Providing *searching* capabilities is an obvious means for locating information. There are numerous Internet search engines such as AltaVista, Lycos, Excite, or InfoSeek. They have smaller siblings for Intranets, some based on the same technology, others coming from older information retrieval roots. The goal of a search is to come up with documents that are *similar* to the query. A query can, for example, be formulated as a listing of terms probably connected by Boolean operators (AND, OR, NOT), or a SQL statement, or a plain English sentence, or a collection of sample documents.

Mapping is a technology to structure, visualize, and manage webs of information. Similar to real maps, graphical maps show readers where they are and where they can go from here, and it gives them an overview of their local and global context. They are thus one of the most flexible, versatile, and user-friendly means for navigation in cyberspace. Humans can easily understand a hierarchical document structure. Almost all printed books are organized hierarchically. Prospective hypertext authors are well advised to employ a hierarchical document structure for a new document. The hierarchical information structure is then made obvious to the users in a map and put at their disposal as their principal navigation aid.

The concept of *guides* and *agents* is popular for navigation and many other areas. The agent metaphor is well understood by humans, because agents simulate human assistants. The systems in this category incorporate artificial intelligence-based techniques derived from the metaphor of agents' assisting human readers in their complex orientation tasks. The agents are implemented in different ways, ranging from simple, hard-wired guides to rule-based agents that are able to react more flexibly to different needs of different users.

Linking, searching, mapping, and agents are the four concepts employed to access information in a knowledge management system. Readers can employ these concepts to access structured, semi-structured, and unstructured information. Figure 5.9 depicts the technical architecture for a Web-based knowledge management system, putting together the pieces discussed above.

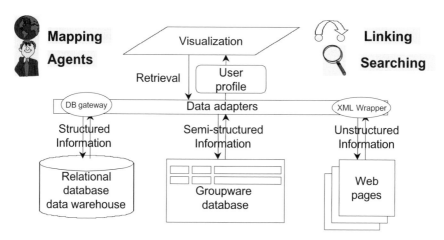

Fig. 5.9 Web knowledge base architecture.

In a knowledge management system, the underlying data can be stored in different formats. Structured data is stored in relational databases and might be condensed in data warehouses. Semi-structured information can, for example, be found in groupware databases like Lotus Notes. Unstructured information comes, for instance, from the corporate Intranet as Web pages. Making this various information sources accessible in a unified interface is a technically demanding task. Data adapters can convert this heterogeneous information into a unified access format: HTML or XML are frequently used for this purpose. Relational database information can be accessed and converted to HTML or XML using a variety of database gateway products. Semi-structured information from a groupware system is converted automatically into HTML format by groupware products like Lotus Notes or Microsoft Exchange. Web HTML pages can be encoded or tagged for better search access by adding an XML wrapper. The visualization component employs the four design concepts for knowledge navigation to optimally visualize the information and make it easily accessible. The more that is known about the structure of the underlying data, the better the visualization of the information can be customized.

We will now look at the four design concepts for knowledge navigation in detail.

5.2.4 Linking

"Pick up your pen, mouse or favorite pointing device and press it on a reference in this document — perhaps to the author's name, organization, or some related work. Suppose you are directly presented with the background material – other papers, the author's coordinates, the organization's address and its entire telephone directory. Suppose each of these documents has the same property of being linked to other original documents all over the world. You would have at your fingertips all you need to know about electronic publishing, high-energy physics or for that matter Asian culture. As you are reading this book on paper, you can only dream, but read on" Tim Berners-Lee *et al.* (1992).

Tim Berners-Lee, the inventor of the Web, has made his dream come true by creating the World Wide Web. In his vision he described the predominant capability of the Web, to jump with one mouse click from one Web page to another. Adding and following links between related documents is one of the main characteristics of the Web. But it is very easy to add too many links to a document, and to get lost in cyberspace by clicking at random at different links. To improve the accessibility of a knowledge base, it is well worth to take one step backwards and look at the various types of links that an author could add to a document. Figure 5.10 displays the different links types. The grey boxes represent single Web pages, connected by different types of links.

- Page links: If a printed document is converted to Web format, page links rebuild the original ordering sequence of the pages and thus reflect the primary sequential reading order as intended by the book author. They connect a particular page with its predecessor and successor and recreate a locally sequential context for the page.
- Hierarchical links: Hierarchical links reflect the logical ordering of the original sections of the document. Because most documents are inherently

5

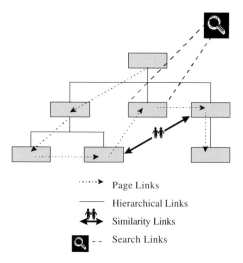

······▶   Page Links

─────   Hierarchical Links

👫   Similarity Links

🔍 --   Search Links

Fig. 5.10   Different link types.

hierarchically structured, hierarchical links are the most powerful means for achieving easily navigable and user-friendly hyperdocuments.

- Similarity links: Similarity links connect documents that have similar contents but are not yet connected by page or hierarchical links. They are frequently computed automatically based on similar terms in different documents and are generated by means of a statistical evaluation of the document collection to be linked.
- Search links: Search links are generated automatically in answer to a query made by the retrieval system.

A well-designed and well-linked web document is using all four of these link types to provide an optimal reading and browsing experience to the reader.

The high dimensionality of a linked hypertext document allows readers many ways of traversing the document. A novice user soon gets overwhelmed by the number of possible ways to read through the document. Guided tours or paths offer a simple mechanism for quickly providing an overview of a hypermedia document. These tools hide the complexity of hypertext by constraining the user to a sequential path. Guided tours are not to be confused with guides described later in the section about guides and agents. The idea of guided tours can be traced back to Vannevar Bush and the origins of hypertext. Bush calls a guided tour a trail and describes it as a sequence of "links through the Memex". The "go next" and "go previous" buttons in each standard Web browser provide simple guided tours.

5.2.5 Searching

To locate well-hidden information in vast information collections, powerful search features are absolutely essential. The advent of large, multimedia digital libraries on the Web has focused attention on retrieving documents consisting of multiple media types, including the traditional focus on textual sources and the increasing emphasis on other media types such as sound, maps, graphics, images, video, etc. Content-based retrieval uses features of multimedia objects in their native form for indexing, storage, and retrieval.

Users can phrase their search query in plain English, as Boolean searches, as a relational SQL statement, or as a collection of sample documents. Afterwards, the retrieval engine performs a similarity computation, matching the query with all the documents in the information collection. Finally, the documents most similar to the query are retrieved and returned to the users (Fig. 5.11).

The most important parameter to measure the success of a query is the precision, i.e. the proportion of retrieved material that is relevant.

Closed document management and groupware systems like Xerox Documentum, Lotus Notes, or Microsoft Exchange have their own search capability built-in. For large, company-wide Intranets, this approach is impractical as:

- There are also documents in other formats accessible on the Intranet, which cannot directly be searched by a proprietary search system.
- There is the question of scalability: searching one million Lotus Notes documents might return too many hits, and the query might take a very long time to execute. The Internet community has addressed this problem with search engines such as AltaVista, Lycos, Excite, or InfoSeek. The search engines send out robots (see below), that go out on the Web and index all documents that they encounter, i.e. the robot builds an index listing all occurrences of a word on the Web pages.

The Web offers information providers and authors great flexibility in implementing their own search subsystems. They can use either Intranet versions of Web search engines such as AltaVista, or employ proprietary information retrieval systems that have been around before the advent of the Web and have been ported to the open Internet standards such as Fulcrum, or OpenText.

Robots

Web robots are software programs that traverse the Web automatically. Robots are sometimes also called Web wanderers, Web crawlers, spiders, or bots, names that are somewhat misleading because they give the impression that the

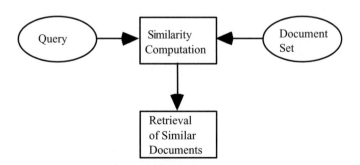

Fig. 5.11   Basic search mechanism.

5

software itself would move between sites like a virus or an autonomous agent. In reality, a robot visits sites by requesting documents from them. Search engines like Lycos, Alta Vista, and InfoSeek are not robots; they are programs that search through information collections gathered by a robot. Robots are used on the Web for different purposes, such as indexing, HTML validation, link validation, "What's New" monitoring, and mirroring.

The most popular application of robots is for gathering Web pages to be indexed for search engines. Indexing robots employ various search strategies to decide what Web sites to visit. In general they start from a historical list of URLs, especially of documents with many links elsewhere, such as server lists, "What's New" pages, and the most popular sites on the Web. Most indexing services also allow Web users to submit URLs manually, which are then added to the historical list of URLs. Using those starting points, a robot selects URLs to visit and index, and to parse and use as a source for new URLs. If an indexing robot knows about a document, it may decide to parse it and insert it into its database. How this is done depends on the robot. Some robots index the HTML titles, or the first few paragraphs; others parse the entire HTML text and index all words, with weighting depending on HTML constructs.

Robots should be used on the Web only by experienced Web programmers because of the risks involved when robots are let loose without considering the consequences. If a robot is implemented improperly, it can overload networks and servers. There are guidelines available for properly implementing robots. And even if a robot is implemented correctly, it can nevertheless be used improperly, resulting in network and server overload. If a robot visits one site too fast in sequence, it can slow down the server, even causing server crashes.

A potential problem with indexing robots is that centralized search databases built by Web-wide indexing robots do not scale easily to millions of documents on millions of sites.

Most robots provide valuable services to the Web community. However, a standard has been established for keeping robots away from certain pages or even blocking them totally from visiting a server. To block a robot from visiting a server, the following two lines need to be placed into the server:

     User-agent: *
     Disallow: /

It is also possible to specify selectively in a special file if certain robots should be prohibited from visiting particular files. Of course, this procedure works only if the robot itself obeys this protocol.

Advanced searching

Any query on a search engine like Altavista, Lycos, Excite, or Infoseek, can easily result in digital diarrhoea – tens of thousands of web pages that are irrelevant. Different strategies have been proposed to provide relief. ARC (automatic resource compiler) (Chakrabarti *et al.*, 1998) has been developed by researchers at Cornell University, the IBM Almaden Research Center, and the University of California at Berkeley. ARC automatically categorizes Web sites, similarly to the way that Yahoo's categorizers do manually.

ARC works by first performing an ordinary Boolean test-based search, for example locating documents that contain the word "diamond" using a search engine such as AltaVista. After generating a quick list of about 200 pages, ARC then expands that set to include documents linked to and from those 200 pages. The step is repeated to obtain a collection of up to 3000 locations. ARC then analyzes the interconnections between those documents, giving higher scores to those pages that are frequently cited, with the assumption that such documents are more useful. One feature of ARC is that it leads to the natural separation of Web sites into communities. A search for information on abortion, for instance, will result in two sets of sites, pro-life and pro-choice, because documents from one group are more likely to link to one another than to pages from the other community. Though clever, ARC is not perfect. A search on a specific topic such as "Martina Hingis" can result in Web pages on the general subject of tennis without any mention of the Swiss tennis star.

The "Google" search engine (www.google.com) also offers search results based on an analysis of the links structure. Its "...PageRank technology interprets a link from page A to page B as a vote, by page A, for page B. Google assesses a page's importance by the votes it receives. But Google looks at more than sheer volume of votes, or links; it also analyzes the page that casts the vote. Votes cast by pages that are themselves 'important' weigh more heavily and help to make other pages 'important' ...".

Another remedy against digital diarrhoea is offered by the Northern Light search engine (www.northernlight.com). Northern Light works similarly to the other search engines like AltaVista, Infoseek, or Excite, but it then clusters tens of thousands of documents returned to a query.

Search results are grouped by similarity in hierarchical folders. In the example of Fig. 5.12, some documents in return to the query "holocaust jew switzerland" were placed in the folder "Special Collection documents", which contains a folder "Jewish Week (news)" which contains folders "Holocaust", "World War II", etc. This gives the reader a hierarchically structured view of an unstructured, *ad hoc* document collection, where the documents are grouped by similarity.

Consequently, some researchers feel that future tools will need to offer a variety of techniques, depending on the type of information desired. Other methods being investigated include morphological and linguistical analyses that might, for example, aid in finding a person's home page, as opposed to articles written about that person. Web Rings are not tools for searching, but linked communities of shared interest, where, for example, hundreds of Web sites about knitting are linked to a virtual ring of Web pages.

Searching semi-structured information

Known structural properties of semi-structured information can be put to use for improved searching in very large information collections. As a consulting company whose core asset is the knowledge of its consultants, PricewaterhouseCoopers heavily invests into building better tools and methods for managing knowledge. PricewaterhouseCoopers' more than 140,000 consultants should be supported in finding and feeding back information into the corporate Intranet. The goal is to make better use of all the information available in the tens of thousands of company-internal Lotus Notes databases. To further that goal, scientists in the PricewaterhouseCoopers Advanced Technology Center in Menlo Park have built a system to make unified searches over the global

Fig. 5.12   Clustered presentation. Sample of Northernlight.com search results.

company-internal Notes network. The problem is, for example, that there are multiple resumé databases, or multiple phone directories. The system needs to be capable of extracting a complete and up-to-date resume, or the current office and home phone numbers of a PricewaterhouseCoopers consultant. To achieve these goals, the system uses the information structure, by, for example, automatically analyzing the names of fields in Notes databases. The system also makes clever guesses by contents of a field, for example drawing the conclusion that a particular field might contain phone numbers because of the numbers in it or that another field might contain company names because it encounters familiar names. To guarantee high-quality search output, human preprocessing is needed: for instance, the data quality of a particular database is manually classified, asserting that a phone number in one database is more likely to be correct than in another.

This system is applied, for example, to automatically condense information about a particular client company, consulting thousands of Notes databases in the process (Fig. 5.13). Another application is the automatic generation of a complete and up-to-date consultant resumé, clipping together pieces from different resumé databases. As management consultants are global nomads, a simple, but non-trivial application is to locate the current office address of a PricewaterhouseCoopers employee.

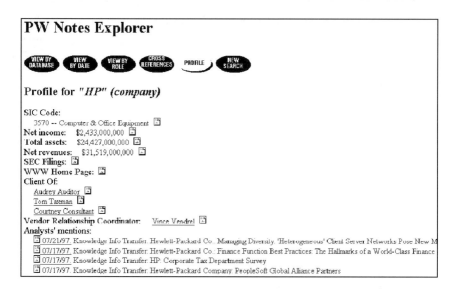

Fig. 5.13   Automatically generated client report.

User profiles and collaborative filtering

User profiles are used for mass customization where the appearance of a system and its interface to the user are adopted according to needs and wishes of the user. An accurate model of the user can also considerably improve the success of a search, as information retrieval systems often lack the capability of adapting their behaviour to different user categories. Naive users, users with a specific background in the search domain, newcomers, and experienced users are all treated the same. Internet bookstore Amazon.com employs a sophisticated searching system, trying to come up with personalized suggestions for new books that the user might be interested in. Amazon's user preference matching works along different facets:

● Instant recommendations: This feature offers recommendations based on past purchases of a registered client.
● BookMatcher: Customers rate some books, then Amazon gives them personalized recommendations.
● MoodMatcher: Books are categorized in generic groups, into books for every occasion and every mood.
● Customer Buzz: These are books that have been recommended by other, like-minded customers.
● If you like this author ... : A customer can select her favourite authors, then Amazon will lead her to other, similar authors.

Firefly is the best-known player in collaborative filtering. Formerly called Agents Inc., it is a spin-off of the Massachusetts Institute of Technology's Media Lab. Its software can suggests films, books or music by quizzing visitors about personal preferences and then comparing those answers to those of people with similar tastes. Firefly's products allow end-users to create profiles

5

of information to be provided to specific Web sites. These sites can maintain and exchange user information when authorized and can provide content based on users' profiles. Microsoft recently acquired Firefly and plans to include Firefly software in the next version of its Site Server Commerce Edition.

5.2.6 Knowledge maps

Geographical maps are a well-known means for orientation in the real world. Their purpose is at least three-fold:

(1) They show readers where they are.
(2) They show readers where they can go from here.
(3) They give readers an overview of their environment.

As Davenport and Pruzak (1997) note, a knowledge map is a guide to knowledge, but it does not contain it. It can be a database, a yellow page dictionary, etc. Developing a knowledge map entails locating knowledge and then publishing some sort of a picture describing where to find it. Davenport and Pruzak speak of knowledge maps in a very broad sense, also including a Rolodex containing the addresses of people knowledgeable in a certain field in their definition of knowledge map. This section discusses the technical realization of knowledge maps. Usually this includes the creation of some graphical visualization representing the knowledge that can be accessed using the map. From the map, readers can jump to the actual pieces of knowledge, those being, for example, an Intranet Web document, a link to some external Web site, a groupware document, or an entry in a legacy database (Fig. 5.14).

Extending the analogy to geographical maps, overview maps of knowledge serve exactly the same purpose:

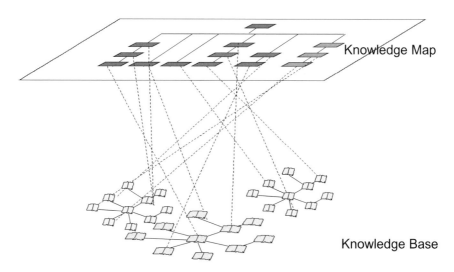

Fig. 5.14   Mapping knowledge.

- The map is always in relation to the actual location of the user in the knowledge management system; it shows users where they are in the document universe. This feature is usually implemented by highlighting the actual location.
- They show readers where they can go from here. Based on the interests of the user the map shows the user other documents of potential interest.
- They try to convey the whole document collection structure in graphical form to the user.

Maps can be used to visualize links, search results, sequential paths, hierarchies, and similarities between documents. A meaningfully structured document can substantially assist in exploring and locating information. Hierarchical structuring, as employed frequently in technical documentation and manuals, is one of the most efficient means of organizing large document collections. There are two ways of imposing a hierarchical document structure:

(1) Ideally, a document is molded into a hierarchical structure during its creation and authoring phase.
(2) It is much harder to impose a hierarchical structure on an existing document collection. Mapping tools attempt to compute a meaningful structure, preferably hierarchical, for any collection of documents.

An electronic table of contents is a straightforward navigation aid that covers a reader's basic needs. Its big advantage lies in its familiarity to the user because it corresponds to similar means for the printed book. Compared to printed books, an electronic table of contents offers improved access by allowing the user to directly jump to the beginning of a chapter by clicking on an entry. Electronic tables of contents are also easily constructed automatically from book manuscripts based on the chapter structure.

Figure 5.15 displays two examples of hierarchical overview maps. The left picture contains a screen shot of the well-known hierarchical directory view of Microsoft Windows, the picture on the right displays one page of a large document in the Microsoft WinWord On-line Layout view. This view displays a

 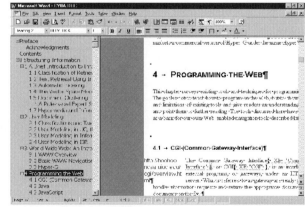

Fig. 5.15 Two examples of hierarchical table of contents overview maps.

hierarchical table of contents of the whole document in the left window frame, clicking on a chapter entry in the table of contents brings up the first page of the chapter in the right frame.

Although humans understand hierarchical views best, there are many opportunities where other views are more appropriate. If large knowledge bases such as a collection of Web documents on a corporate Intranet are visualized in a straightforward manner by connecting all the links between the documents, meaningless spiderweb views such as the one displayed in Fig. 5.16 are the results.

To come up with better ways to visualize large knowledge bases, many clever layout algorithms and visualization tools have been developed in the last few years.

Web mapping tools

The multidimensional structure of the Web is ideally suited for visualization by mapping. There have been different approaches suggested, and there are at least a dozen commercial companies selling tools for "Web cartography." These tools are all optimally suited for creating knowledge maps.

An ideal knowledge map offers not only a generic overview of the whole hyperdocument, but is also able to offer a personalized view of the document based on the preferences of the user. This means that the system has to keep at least two knowledge bases about the user:

(1) User profile. The user profile contains data about the user's interests and preferences. These data items are manipulated directly or indirectly by the user.
(2) Reading history of the user. As the map tracks the path of the reader through the document, an advanced version should be able to modify a

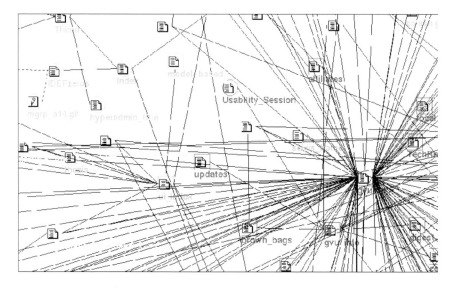

Fig. 5.16   Web spiderweb view (source: Georgia Tech).

stereotypic user model concerning user capabilities and user preferences by analyzing the reading behaviour. The system would then be able to make better guesses about the interests of the reader.

The user profile is thus of fundamental importance for a flexible and informative overview map.

Figure 5.17 emphasizes the role of the user profile for the automatic generation of customized maps. Each user looks through a different, personalized "lens" on the same knowledge base. The personal profile stores personal needs and requirements, enabling the ability to filter out unwanted information and providing a focus on the information most relevant to each user.

The developers of the systems described below have each chosen a different approach to provide this personalized filtering mechanism.

Inxight's hyperbolic trees

Inxight (www.inxight.com), a spin-off of Xerox PARC, is licensing different visualization modules to illustrious clients such as Microsoft or the *Wall Street Journal*. Its focus is solely on various ways of displaying large information spaces, without doing any processing of the underlying information. Contrarily to the other tool vendors described in this section, it is not providing any indexing, querying, or clustering subsystems. Inxight has come up with visualization concepts like cone trees, three-dimensional rooms, or perspective walls. Its most popular concept is the hyperbolic tree, a spider web-like hierarchical display that shows major topics connected by lines to related topics and subtopics (Fig. 5.18). Users can drag a topic to the centre of the screen, and focus on a set of related concepts. Users can then click on topics to jump to the underlying document.

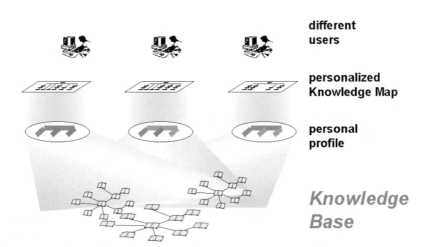

different users

personalized Knowledge Map

personal profile

Knowledge Base

5

Fig. 5.17 Role of the user profile for personalized knowledge maps.

Fig. 5.18   Hyperbolic tree of the Louvre Web site.

Cartia's ThemeScape

Cartia is developing ThemeScape, an application that automatically organizes document collections based on their content. The result is an interactive landscape of information, a topographical map that shows what is inside of documents and web pages.

Every document and web page is organized onto a topographical map based on the information it contains (Fig. 5.19). Topics for which there are many documents appear as peaks on the map. Topics that are similar in nature are close together on the map. Valleys divide topics that are not closely related. Search capabilities highlight relevant documents directly on the map.

ThemeScape requires no manual categorizations or document tagging; a "harvester" processes any combination of document directories or web sites, reading in the documents and organizing them onto the interactive landscape of information.

SemioMap

SemioMap (www.semio.com) consists of three parts: Semio Builder, Semio Taxonomy, and SemioMap itself. The core engine is Semio Builder. It automatically extracts meaningful concepts from text and identifies the relationships between these ideas.

Semio Taxonomy automatically creates browse-able, searchable directories for Intranets and web sites. It generates a taxonomy (structure) and then

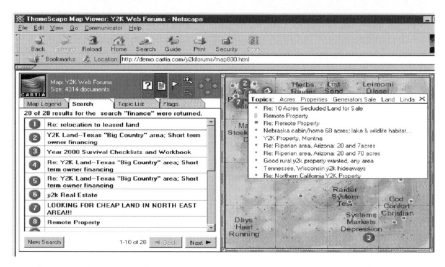

Fig. 5.19 ThemeScape of a Year 2000 map, visualizing search results on word "finance".

categorizes the content appropriately. The browse-able directory has a multi-level structure that includes thesaurus-like links. These links cross-reference related parts of the directory. This cross-referencing capability matches thought patterns, not only hierarchically, but also across concepts.

SemioMap creates visual, navigable representations of text-based content (Fig. 5.20). Information is displayed in a manner similar to Inxight's hyperbolic trees. Topics are depicted as galaxies on a starry background

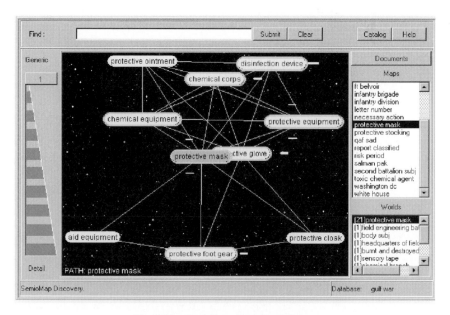

Fig. 5.20 SemioMap about the Gulf war.

with lines connecting to related topics. Users can quickly find the specific areas of interest to them, because the concepts are displayed "in context" with related concepts. Users can also drag topics around to rearrange perspectives of the information. The maps uncover interesting or new links that are not apparent otherwise.

Autonomy's knowledge management tool suite

Autonomy (www.autonomy.com) is marketing a tool suite for creating knowledge maps. Called Knowledge Server, Knowledge Update, and Knowledge Builder, Autonomy's software tools automate knowledge management by automatically cross-referencing, linking, categorizing and summarizing information. Its tools aggregate content from corporate information repositories in many different formats.

Knowledge Server automates the accurate categorization of large volumes of both internal and external information. It automatically inserts hypertext links to related information whenever a user retrieves a document, e-mail message, or web page. Because links are created at the time of retrieval, they are always kept up to date. It facilitates finding information by suggesting relevant sources. It also automatically profiles the expertise of all users by analyzing the documents that they produce as well as the information they research on-line.

The KnowledgeServer Visualizer (Fig. 5.21) presents an easy-to-navigate visual interface that automatically presents a unified view of disparate data sources across the enterprise, including e-mail messages, word processing files, PowerPoint presentations, etc. It also shows users how information is related.

The KnowledgeServer Explorer (Fig. 5.22) automates the classification into clusters of information. It allows users to navigate in search results by clusters

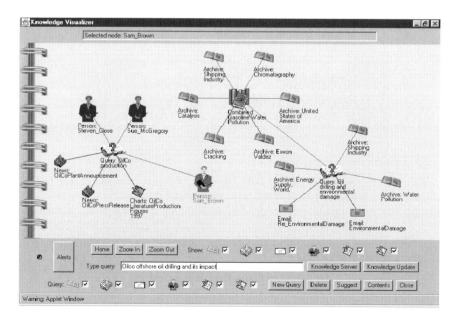

Fig. 5.21   KnowledgeServer visualization.

of information, created automatically to provide a visual interface of "islands" of knowledge. This automated process is accomplished by using a sophisticated cluster analysis algorithm.

Knowledge Update eliminates the need to surf the Internet and Intranet just to stay up-to-date on developments that are relevant. This module monitors specified Internet and Intranet sites, news feeds and internal repositories containing Lotus Notes, HTML, word processing files, PDF files, and many others. It creates a personalized report informing individual users of developments that are relevant to them. Autonomy's software is also capable of preventing on-line access to any category of content that an organization deems inappropriate.

Perspecta

Perspecta, an MIT Media Lab spin-off, encompasses both organizing and presenting database information. It organizes large amounts of information and displays it as a detailed chart, with multiple links that users can click on to see the information organized. The Dynamic Query Server, at the heart of the system, provides a scalable, dynamic *ad hoc* query environment for high volumes of information and large numbers of users. The Dynamic Query Server also includes additional capabilities surrounding those requests, in context, such as related information, alternative queries, and suggestions for refining or generalizing the result set. Perspecta's software tool suite SDK enables fast development and maintenance of a Perspecta-powered application.

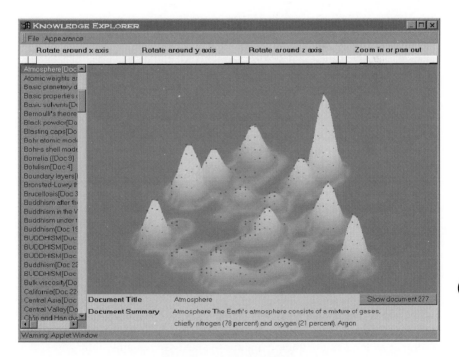

Fig. 5.22 Knowledge Explorer.

Interactive Web applications can then be built on top of large company databases using this presentation software development kit.

All of these knowledge mapping applications provide unconventional GUIs, far more powerful than the conventional, text-based search interfaces of older information retrieval systems. Nevertheless, the products listed in this section differ greatly in their degree of ease-of-use, performance over a network, scalability, and openness. The Inxight Hyperbolic tree has been integrated into mass-market products like Microsoft's FrontPage and is relatively well polished. Products like SemioMap or Perspecta are at the other end of the range, requiring an expert user for adding additional documents to the database. Their ways of visualizing information also need more getting used and are therefore better suited for specialized users like librarians, or professional information seekers and knowledge discoverers. Cartia's The-meScape and Autonomy's Knowledge Tool Suite cover the middle ground, providing relatively easy-to-use navigation interfaces. They also offer indexing and clustering back ends that can be used in their standard settings by moderately computer-literate users. While I am convinced that visual navigation systems like the ones described in this section will become ubiquitous for knowledge mapping, it remains to be seen which ones of these systems will gain the widest market acceptance.

5.2.7 Agents

In a similar way to the knowledge mapping concepts previously discussed, agents can assist readers in following links, conducting searches, constructing sequential paths, navigating in hierarchies, and recognizing similarities. More generally, agents can be used to filter information, to match people with similar interest, or to automate repetitive behaviour.

Sometimes agents are further divided into "simpler" guides and "true" agents. Although both guides and agents assist readers in exploring large information spaces, agents embody a notion of autonomous behaviour as well as "intelligence", while guides represent a human-like metaphor to assist in the navigation task. Contrary to guided tours that take readers through a predefined path, guides are more flexible. They simulate a human guide, which helps the user in orienting in unknown territory. The autonomous version of the guide, the agent, even tries to work out the needs of the user and offer solutions based on this assessment. Guides and agents need not necessarily be represented on the computer screen by a virtual person, although for a computer-illiterate user, this interface may be more obvious than an abstract text-based representation. Compared with agents, guides are more restricted and less autonomous. The guide idea stresses the human-like representation, but contrary to agents, guides do not contain real content knowledge about the information they manage (Table 5.1).

An agent is more powerful than a guide, but in practice guides frequently are hard-wired to show agent-like behaviour. The user will not notice the difference as long as the underlying knowledge base remains static and is not modified by the user.

Table 5.1 Guides versus agents

Guides	Agents
Simple form of agents	Autonomous software entities
Present document selection based on index	Respond dynamically to user's goals, preferences, learning style, knowledge
Assume role of guideposts and storytellers	Require some degree of "intelligence"

Guides: Orientation assistants

Guides provide a familiar interface to readers by simulating a virtual creature on the screen that assists them in their orientation task. Guides can be as simple as Simon the storyteller in Brøderbound's animated children's book of Aesop's *The Tortoise and the Hare*. The pictures in Fig. 5.23 display Simon introducing the different animated pages of the children's book. Simon exhibits hard-wired behaviour; in the opening sequence to each page, he introduces the story of the page in a canned movie. Nevertheless, Simon offers an easy-to-use navigation feature that can be understood even by 3-year-olds.

The main goal of using guides is to provide a simpler navigation interface than a complex hypertext map or a conventional query interface. Guides also succeed in merging browsing and search into one single metaphor. Deliberate personification of the navigation interface can result in increased engagement of the user. Particular care has to be taken not to annoy more experienced users, because once users know what they are looking for, they might see a guide as an obstruction rather than help. This problem can be addressed by monitoring the user's behaviour. Once the system has guessed the user's intention, guides can offer to provide the information they think the user is searching. Guides at this level of sophistication are starting to behave like agents as described in the next section and are thus on a gradual scale between the two concepts.

Real agents

Agents are currently a "hot topic" in the Internet community and an ongoing area of research. This section briefly illustrates the state of the art and outlines the potential of agent technology to support managing knowledge.

5

Fig. 5.23 The guide Simon in *The Tortoise and the Hare*.

The use of agents as a new interface model for human–computer interaction was first proposed by Alan Kay. He also called agents "soft robots".

"The model-building capabilities of the computer should enable mindlike processes to be built and should allow designers to create flexible "agents". These agents will take on their owner's goals, confer about strategies (asking questions of users as well as answering their queries) and, by reasoning, fabricate goals of their own" (Kay, 1991).

In the literature three somewhat redundant different types of agents are distinguished:

(1) Autonomous agents – programs that travel between sites, deciding on their own when to move and what to do (e.g. General Magic's Telescript or Agent-Tcl agents). They can travel only between servers that are set up to handle agents and are currently not widespread on the Internet.
(2) Intelligent agents – programs that help users interactively to accomplish a task, such as choosing a product or guiding a user through form-filling or a search. The wizards in Windows 98 or the office assistants in Microsoft Office 97 are simple versions of such agents. Their "intelligence" is in fact quite limited, as they are best at doing a well-defined task in a limited domain. As with most AI applications, vaguely defined tasks requiring common-sense knowledge are ill suited for intelligent agents. This is currently the most popular category of agents.
(3) User-agents – programs that perform mostly networking tasks for a user, such as e-mail user-agents like Qualcomm's Eudora (http://www.qualcomm.com/), which filter a user's e-mail based on her or his interests.

Table 5.2 contains a partial listing of possible tasks that can be done by an agent on behalf of the human user.

One obvious use of the agent concept is for navigation, localization, and filtering of information. Contrary to guides, agents are autonomous software entities that make choices and execute actions on behalf of the user. They incorporate the knowledge to find and present information by responding dynamically to the user's changing goals, preferences, learning style, and knowledge. To succeed in this task, agents need some sort of intelligence. In particular, they require knowledge about the structure and contents of the underlying information. This leads to the conclusion that structured information as in AI knowledge bases like CYC is particularly well suited to being managed by agents. For agents to grant access to unstructured information, this information has to be structured at least internally. For the agent prototypes available so far, most of the document structure has either

Table 5.2 Types of tasks suitable for an agent (Laurel *et al.*, 1990)

Information	Work	Learning	Entertainment
Navigation and browsing	Reminding	Coaching	Playing against
Information retrieval	Programming	Tutoring	Playing with
Sorting and organizing	Scheduling	Providing Help	Performing
Filtering	Advising		

been generated by manually structuring unstructured documents or by limiting the functionality of agents to semi-structured information.

The behaviour and properties of an agent must be made visible to the user. For some agents, a textual representation is completely sufficient – in Weizenbaum's famous ELIZA program, where the computer simulates a psychoanalyst (Weizenbaum, 1976) its bodiless phrases may have been its greatest strength. Frequently, agents that have human-like traits are particularly well suited to make the internal properties of the agent obvious to the user. The ALIVE project at the MIT Media Lab (http://alive.www. media.mit.edu/ projects/alive) offers a new level of immersion to the user employing virtual reality (VR) technologies. It is one of the most advanced agent projects with respect to the human–computer interface. The user can interact with autonomous, intelligent agents in the form of virtual creatures (such as the dog in Fig. 5.24) without being constrained by VR devices such as headsets, goggles, or special sensing equipment. The system is based on the so-called magic mirror metaphor: ALIVE users see their own image on a large TV screen as if in a mirror. Autonomous, animated characters join the user's own image in the reflected world.

Commercial available agents are much simpler. In fact, most so-called Internet agents are not much more than a Web robot, which periodically goes out on the Web to collect an index of topics of interest to the user. The Autonomy Knowledge Update and the ThemeScape Harvester described in the previous section about knowledge mapping both work that way. Another typical representative of such an agent-based system is Verity's Agent Server.

Fig. 5.24 Human interacting with a virtual creature in MIT Media Lab's ALIVE project.

5

Verity AgentServer

Verity, an established vendor of information retrieval products (www.verity.com), is also selling an Internet search agent. Agent Server actively monitors information sources across the Internet and Intranet and automatically filters and delivers personalized information to users, based on their content and delivery preferences. The Agent Server enables users to build their own personal agents that monitor the selected Intranet and Internet resources continually, including documents, e-mail, discussion groups, corporate databases and newswires. Agents notify users proactively when information matching their interest profiles is discovered.

Verity agents employ concept-based queries to ensure only relevant information is delivered to the user. Relevance ranking is automatically applied to retrieved contents, enabling users to gauge the value of delivered information. To customize information delivery further, users can set relevancy thresholds and receive only the most pertinent information or more general matches.

The future: agent-based workflow over the Internet

Contrary to guides, agents react based on an analysis of the real contents of the document. The behaviour of agents is defined by rules. But there is still a long way to go until agents will take over the daily duties that we don't want to do anymore, and will, for example, go out to search the Internet autonomously for the book that we did not find in our local library.

Currently, leading computer scientists as well as the software industry predict a great future for agents. They are even considered one of the "silver bullets" of the software industry. In the future, besides being used for information collection and filtering, agent-based concepts and tools can be applied in many other areas. Transportable agents might migrate from one machine to the other, executing their tasks on behalf of the user. Application areas will cover:

- Information-gathering agents, trying to locate that particular piece of information that the agent's owner is interested in.
- Shopping agents visiting one virtual shopping mall after the other, trying to strike the best deal for their owner.
- Order processing agents doing menial tasks, such as processing a procurement order, carrying out a financial transaction, or doing all the paperwork involved when hiring a new employee.

To be successful in these tasks, important properties need to be added to today's agents. They need to be made trustworthy to be able to carry money to buy on behalf of their owner.

Agents are by their very nature stateless, which means that no central authority knows about all agents all the time. But an agent's owner would like to know what happened to his agent if the agent does not return in a timely fashion. This means that agents also need to be made more reliable. If an agent dies, his actions so far should at least be known, or even better be undone.

5.3 Critical knowledge management success factors for e-business transformation

To successfully transform a business into an e-business, sharing of knowledge must be supported by the right IT tools. Contrary to business process automation by packageware, there are *no out-of-the box systems to create knowledge management frameworks*. Tools and concepts for mapping of knowledge, for the navigation and visualization of information are available, but it is still a manual task to create the user-friendly, easy-to-use knowledge management system enabling each employee of a company to find the information and knowledge to best perform his or her job.

First of all, in order to transform a business, a company needs to understand how its current business works. This knowledge is in the form of process knowledge about its business processes, and domain knowledge, about the general business area. For the *assessment of current business processes*, tools like the MIT Process Handbook can provide useful assistance. To transform the business, best practice e-business processes can then be compared to the "as is" processes of the company stored in the handbook.

An ideal knowledge management system should be a tool that operates on structured, semi-structured and unstructured documents, is capable of giving users an overview of their field of interest, offers guidance on what to do next, and gives a graphical overview of the most relevant pieces of information in reply to a query. The tools described above provide the basic building blocks to build such a system: They operate on *structured as well as unstructured data* without the need for manual preprocessing, they create an *overview map* of the knowledge domain to be explored, they display the most *relevant information* based on the *user's interests*, they provide *sequential and hierarchical navigation*, and they offer *options of what the reader can do next*.

5.4 Conclusions

The companies that consciously manage their knowledge will be prosperous in the e-business economy. This means that a company must build up a culture of knowledge sharing, where sharing knowledge with co-workers is encouraged, and knowledge hoarders are punished. Of course, on the technological side, knowledge should be made accessible and shared over the Intranet. Companies that are prepared to *give away a part of their own knowledge to attract customers* and to create new business opportunities will be the most successful. This also means that companies should be ready to cooperate with competitors, integrating their competitors' offerings into their own, adding value to their own products.

I have told you that your company will profit enormously if it embraces e-business early and wholeheartedly. I have given many arguments for e-business transformation, and have shown numerous examples of companies that have been tremendously successful by being early adopters. I encourage

5

every company to jump on the e-business bandwagon, the sooner the better! Timing is critical, and the winner takes all. Playing catch-up to the leaders in a field has been shown to be extremely costly for the companies that have had to do it. e-Business impacts all business areas. In the area of design and production, new products and services will be created based on Internet technology, and existing products will be produced much more efficiently using this new medium. In the area of marketing and selling, it will be much easier to build customer loyalty and to reach new markets. In the area of management and decision making, companies that embrace the new technologies early will get a unique chance to achieve market leadership. They will be capable of optimizing business processes by harnessing emerging e-business technologies. They can also better manage internal and external risks by using the Internet wisely. In the area of learning and change, they can enhance their investment into human capital by nurturing a culture of knowledge sharing.

Come and join the e-business leaders. The journey has just begun!

References and further reading

Berners-Lee, T., Cailliau, R., Groff, J. and Pollermann, B. (1992) *World-Wide Web: The Information Universe*. CERN, Geneva, Switzerland.

Bush, V. (1945) As we may think. *Atlantic Monthly* 176, No. 1. Reprinted in Greif, I. (ed.) (1988) *Computer-Supported Cooperative Work: A Book of Readings*. Morgan Kaufmann Publishers, San Mateo, CA.

Cai, T., Gloor, P. and Nog, S. (1996) DartFlow: A Workflow Management System on the Web using Transportable Agents. Technical Report PCS-TR96–283, Department of Computer Science, Dartmouth College.

Chakrabarti, S., Dom, B., Gibson, D., Kleinberg, J., Raghavan, P. and Rajagopalan, S. (1998) Automatic resource list compilation by analyzing hyperlink structure and associated text. *Proc. 7th International World Wide Web Conference*, 1998 (http://decweb.ethz.ch/WWW7/1898/com1898.htm).

Coen, M. (1994) SodaBot: A Software Agent Environment and Construction System. MIT AI Lab Technical Report 1493, 4 June.

Coen, M. (1997) Building brains for rooms: designing distributed software agents. In *Proc. 9th Conference on Innovative Applications of Artificial Intelligence* (IAAI97), Providence, RI.

Davenport, T. H. and Prusak, L. (1997) *Working Knowledge: How Organizations Manage What They Know*. Harvard Business School Press, Cambridge, MA.

Digital Equipment (1995) LinkWorks White Paper 7/9/95 (www.digital.com/info/linkworks/).

Dertouzos, M. L. (1997) *What Will Be: How the New World of Information Will Change Our Lives*. Harper Edge, HarperCollins, New York.

Downes, L. and Mui, C. (1998) *Unleashing the Killer App: Digital Strategies for Market Dominance*. Harvard Business School Press, Cambridge, MA.

Fox, R. (1999) News track. *Communication of the ACM*, **42**, 5, 9.

Gallaugher, J. (1999) Challenging the new conventional wisdom of net commerce strategies. *Communications of the ACM*, **42**, 7, 27–29.

Glass, R. (1999) The realities of software technology payoffs. *Communications of the ACM*, **42**, 2, 74–79.

Gloor, P. (1997) Elements of hypermedia design: techniques for navigation and visualization in cyberspace. Birkhäuser, Cambridge MA (also available on the Web at www.birkhauser.com/hypermedia/).

Gloor, P. and Dynes, S. (1998) Cybermap – visually navigating the Web. *Journal of Visual Languages and Computing*, **9**, 319–336.

Gloor, P. and Uhlmann, P. (1999) The impact of e-commerce on developing countries. *Proc. BIS '99*, Poznan, Poland, 14–16 April.

Glushko, R. J., Tenenbaum, J. M. and Meltzer, B. (1999) An XML framework for agent-based e-commerce. *Communications of the ACM*, **42**, 3, 106–110.

Goleman, D. P. (1997) *Emotional Intelligence*. Bantam Books, New York.

Gray, R., Kotz, D., Nog, S., Rus, D. and Cybenko, G. (1996) Mobile agents for mobile computing. Technical Report: PCS-TR96–285, Department of Computer Science, Dartmouth College.

Hammer, M. and Champy, J. (1993) *Reengineering the Corporation.* HarperCollins, New York.

Herrnstein, R. J. and Murray C. (contributor) (1996) *The Bell Curve: Intelligence and Class Structure in American Life.* Free Press, New York.

Johnson G. (1999) Searching for the essence of the World Wide Web. *The New York Times*, 11 April (http://www.nytimes.com/library/review/041199internet-ecosystem-review.html).

Kay, A. (1991) Computers, networks and education. *Scientific American*, **265**, 3, September, 138–148.

Kraut, R. Patterson, M., Lundmark, V., Kiesler, S, Mukophadhyay, T. and Scherlis, W. (1998). Internet paradox: A social technology that reduces social involvement and psychological well-being? *American Psychologist*, **53**, 9, 1017–1031. Homenet Project (1997) Internet paradox: a social technology that reduces social involvement and psychological well-being (http://homenet.andrew.cmu.edu/progress/).

Laurel, B., Oren, T. and Don, A. (1992) Issues in multimedia interface design: Media integration and interface agents. In Blattner, M. M. and Dannenberg, R. B. (eds) *Multimedia Interface Design.* ACM Press, New York, 53–64. (Originally from *CHI '90*, ACM Press, New York, 1990, 133–139.)

Leymann, F., Roller, D. and Vogt, E. (1995) White Paper: Workflow Management. IBM Software Solutions Division, German Software Development Laboratory, Boeblingen.

Lyytinen, K. and Goodman, S. (1999) Finland: The unknown soldier on the IT front. *Communications of the ACM*, **42**, 3, 13–17.

Malone, T., Crowston, K., Lee, J. and Pentland, B. (1993) Tools for inventing organizations: Toward a handbook of organizational processes. Sloan School Technical Report WP # 3562–93.

Malone, T. W., Crowston, K., Lee, J., Pentland, B., Dellarocas, C., Wyner, G., Quimby, J., Osborn, C. and Bernstein, A. (1997) *Tools for Inventing Organizations: Toward a Handbook of Organizational Processes.* MIT Sloan School of Business, Cambridge, MA (http://ccs.mit.edu/papers/CCSWP198/index.html).

Malone, T. W., Crowston, K. G., Lee, J., Pentland, B., Dellarocas, C., Wyner, G., Quimby, J., Osborn, C. S., Bernstein, A., Herman, G., Klein, M., and O'Donnell, E. (1999) Tools for inventing organizations: Toward a handbook of organizational processes. *Management Science*, **45**, 3, 425–443 (http://www.ccs.mit.edu/21c/mgtsci/)).

Müller, J. P., Wooldridge, M. J. and Jennings, N. R. (1997) *Intelligent Agents III, Agent Theories, Architectures, and Languages. Lecture Notes in Artificial Intelligence*, 1193, Springer, Berlin.

Nielsen, J. (1999) User interface directions for the Web. *Communications of the ACM*, **42**, 1, 65–72.

Weizenbaum, J. (1976) *Computer Power and Human Reason: From Judgement to Calculation.* W.H. Freeman, San Fransisco, CA.

Workflow Management Coalition, International Organization for the Development and Promotion of Workflow Standards (1995) Glossary. Workflow Management Coalition, Avenue Marcel Thiry 204, 1200 Brussels, Belgium.

World Bank (1998). *World Economic Report.* World Bank, Washington, DC.

Xerox Palo Alto Research Center (1999) Internet Ecologies Area (http://www.parc.xerox.com/istl/groups/iea/).

Index